The World in a Classroom

Multilingual Matters

Attitudes and Language
COLIN BAKER
Breaking the Boundaries
EUAN REID and HANS H. REICH (eds)
Citizens of This Country: The Asian British
MARY STOPES-ROE and RAYMOND COCHRANE
Community Languages: A Handbook
BARBARA M. HORVATH and PAUL VAUGHAN
Continuing to Think: The British Asian Girl
BARRIE WADE and PAMELA SOUTER
Education of Chinese Children in Britain:
A Comparative Study with the United States of America
LORNITA YUEN-FAN WONG
Fluency and Accuracy
HECTOR HAMMERLY
Key Issues in Bilingualism and Bilingual Education
COLIN BAKER
Language, Culture and Cognition
LILLIAM MALAVÉ and GEORGES DUQUETTE (eds)
Language Distribution Issues in Bilingual Schooling
R. JACOBSON and C. FALTIS (eds)
Language Policy Across the Curriculum
DAVID CORSON
Life in Language Immersion Classrooms
ELIZABETH B. BERNHARDT (ed.)
Linguistics and Communicative Competence
CHRISTINA BRATT-PAULSTON
Minority Education: From Shame to Struggle
T. SKUTNABB-KANGAS and J. CUMMINS (eds)
Opportunity and Constraints of Community Language Teaching
SJAAK KROON
School to Work in Transition in Japan
KAORI OKANO
Schooling in a Plural Canada
JOHN MALLEA
Sociolinguistic Perspectives on Bilingual Education
CHRISTINA BRATT PAULSTON
Story as Vehicle
EDIE GARVIE

Please contact us for the latest book information:
Multilingual Matters Ltd,
Frankfurt Lodge, Clevedon Hall
Victoria Road, Clevedon,
Avon BS21 7SJ, England

MULTILINGUAL MATTERS 87
Series Editor: Derrick Sharp

The World in a Classroom

Language in Education in Britain and Canada

Viv Edwards and Angela Redfern

MULTILINGUAL MATTERS LTD
Clevedon • Philadelphia • Adelaide

For Henderson Hope

Library of Congress Cataloging in Publication Data

Edwards, Viv
The World in a Classroom: Language in Education in Britain and Canada/
Viv Edwards and Angela Redfern.
p. cm. (Multilingual Matters: 87)
Includes bibliographical references and index.
1. Education, Bilingual–Great Britain. 2. Education, Bilingual–Canada.
3. English language–Study and teaching–Great Britain–Foreign speakers.
4. English language–Study and teaching–Canada–Foreign speakers.
I. Redfern, Angela. II. Title. III. Series: Multilingual Matters (Series): 87.
LC3736.G6E34   1992
371.97′00941–dc20

British Library Cataloguing in Publication Data

A CIP catalogue record for this book is available from the British Library.

ISBN 1-85359-159-9 (hbk)
ISBN 1-85359-158-0 (pbk)

Multilingual Matters Ltd

UK: Frankfurt Lodge, Clevedon Hall, Victoria Road, Clevedon, Avon BS21 7SJ.
USA: 1900 Frost Road, Suite 101, Bristol, PA 19007, USA.
Australia: P.O. Box 6025, 83 Gilles Street, Adelaide, SA 5000, Australia.

Printed and bound in Great Britain by WBC Print Ltd, Bridgend.

Contents

Acknowledgements

The starting point for this book was an award in 1990 from the Canadian Government to examine multicultural policy and practice in Canada. Our field work was based on a Board of Education in Ontario, which we have called the Ferndale Board in order to preserve the confidentiality of all those who spoke to us so candidly about the challenges and the problems which they faced. We would like to express our gratitude to educational administrators, school principals, teachers, school–home liaison personnel and community workers, both for their initial willingness to talk to us and to allow us to observe them at work, and for the helpful comments which they later made on various drafts of the book.

The role which Mary Fuller played in this project deserves special mention. She played an important part in planning the fieldwork and was part of the original team which visited Canada. While we collected data on language issues, language policy and resources, she concentrated on the development of multicultural policy. We would like to acknowledge the very careful attention which she paid in commenting on various drafts of the book.

Thanks, too, to Jill Bourne, Jim Cummins and Woll Redfern for their very helpful comments on the manuscript.

Viv Edwards
Angela Redfern

1 The World in a Classroom

Demographic changes in the last few decades have had important implications for all aspects of life in many countries. Population movement has always been a fact of life. The scale of such movement in the second half of the twentieth century, however, has been unprecedented. London, New York, Toronto and Melbourne are among the centres which attract settlers from every continent. 'The Global Village', 'the interdependence of nations' and 'the world in a city' are all expressions which have achieved the status of clichés in recent years. None the less, they underline a new reality which we ignore at our peril.

To what extent have receiving countries been prepared for the consequences of immigration policies motivated more by economic factors than the desire to welcome newcomers? What kind of reception has awaited migrants—adults and children? How have the education systems of the countries of settlement responded to the challenge of meeting the needs of diverse populations? This book attempts to address some of these questions for Canada and Britain. In particular, we wish to look at the challenges of linguistic and cultural diversity for schools, teachers, educational administrators and policy makers.

It is important to make clear at the outset, however, we are concerned with multilingualism rather than the societal bilingualism which has long been a feature of life in Canada and Britain. Canada is a country in which there are two 'charter peoples' – the English and the French – and attempts to safeguard the distinctiveness of the minority Francophone community have given rise to tensions which have remained unresolved for over 200 years. Similarly Welsh and Gaelic-speaking minorities continue to assert their rights to use their mother tongues within a UK context. The focus for the present volume, however, is the multilingualism created by immigration from many different parts of the world during the post-war period. For this reason, almost exclusive emphasis will be placed on Ontario, the province which receives by far the highest proportion of immigrants to Canada, and on England which has served a similar role in relation to the UK.

1

Comparative accounts of different multi-ethnic societies (cf. Bagley, 1986; Solomon, 1988, 1989) are a growing feature of the research literature and underline the international dimension of issues which, for far too long, have been viewed in isolation. The histories of Canada and Britain share many points of similarity, but also many differences. This makes an interesting starting point for comparison. Do local conditions make for quite different perceptions of and responses to needs, or have similar approaches been used in both countries? Since large-scale immigration of 'visible minorities' to Britain pre-dates immigration to Canada by almost twenty years, to what extent have Canadian educators been able to learn from the mistakes and achievements of British schools and teachers faced with similar challenges? And, by the same token, will British teachers be able to learn from solutions arrived at by Canadian teachers approaching the question with fresh eyes? The answers to these questions are of interest well beyond the shores of Canada and Britain.

The opportunity to look closely at developments in Canada is extremely interesting for British educators. There have been very few attempts in the post-war period to document educational responses to diversity – at the level of central government, local education authorities (LEAs) and schools. This state of affairs derives in part from the traditionally decentralised nature of British education where government attempts to influence practice through a system of financial inducements and general advice in pamphlets and directives rather than through the formulation of explicit policy on multicultural education. Given the lack of leadership from central government, it is not surprising that attempts to monitor and evaluate developments have been limited in number and in scope. And there has been relatively little attempt to document and explore the perceptions of classroom teachers (for a notable recent exception to this trend, see Levine, 1990a).

Teachers' perceptions are fundamental to many of the themes which we will be considering in the course of this book, including the attempt to move the teaching of English as a second language from segregated classes to the mainstream. The opportunity to explore the reactions of Canadian teachers and administrators currently involved in this process of change, and to relate these reactions to those of British educators to the same challenges is exciting. From a British perspective, it offers the chance to look with greater insight at a range of issues which have received far too low a profile in the UK. From a Canadian perspective, the comparison of current developments in North America with recent history in the UK can throw interesting light on situations which are often perplexing, seldom straightforward.

The Ferndale Board of Education

The main source of Canadian data – other than published accounts – were visits in the spring of 1989 and 1990 to a Board of Education in Ontario, referred to throughout this book as the Ferndale Board in order to protect the identity of the teachers and central support staff who provided us with information. The visits were extremely well-timed. The Board had just taken an important policy decision to move the delivery of ESL from segregated classes to the mainstream. It was thus a time of change, marked both by excitement and anxieties as to the effects which these changes would have on teachers and children.

It must be said at the outset that the Ferndale Board of Education has not always been in the vanguard of educational change. The policy and practice of many of the Metropolitan Toronto boards of education, for instance, have often been more advanced. The Ferndale Board, however, was an interesting choice for a number of reasons. It allowed the opportunity to look closely at change in progress. Although a number of years behind certain other boards of education in some respects, it was currently addressing issues which had yet to make an impact on many boards elsewhere. There was also evidence that key personnel were taking steps to inform themselves about relevant developments both abroad and in Canada. While we make no claims that the Ferndale Board is representative either of Ontario or other parts of Canada, there can be little doubt that the issues which were emerging as important for teachers, administrators and policy makers in Ferndale at the time of our field study will continue to be matters of concern for education in Ontario and many other places for years to come.

We were able to spend time observing teachers and classrooms in elementary and secondary schools. We were also able to interview a very wide range of people involved in education in Ferndale: librarians, class teachers at elementary and secondary levels, principals, vice-principals, English as a Second Language (ESL) teachers, heritage language teachers and consultants, school community liaison assistants, ESL consultants, supervisory officers, trustees and the Director of Education. We are indebted to all those who gave willingly of their time, and on whose experience and insights we draw.

References to Ferndale throughout this report are best thought of as a snapshot. They represent the preoccupations and practices of one board of education at a very crucial point in time. The situation at the Ferndale Board, as elsewhere, is clearly a dynamic one. It is important, therefore, to stress that we have set out to examine the issues which presented themselves as important at one particular period in time. The examples and the commentary which we provide are not intended in any way as representative either of the Ferndale Board at the time of publication, or of other boards across Ontario. They do, however, give a very valuable insight into the scale and complexity of the changes which are necessary to meet the needs of linguistically and culturally diverse school populations in Canada and in Britain.

A note on terminology

Many aspects of the organisation and delivery of education in Canada and the UK are quite different. Even when dealing with essentially the same phenomena, quite different vocabulary is often employed. For instance, Canadians talk of heritage languages while the British teach community languages. Canadian schools are organised around boards of education, while local education authorities (LEAs) fulfil the same function in Britain. There is a similar divergence in vocabulary for certain ethnic groups. Canadians talk of east Indians; the British refer to south Asians. Various terms have been used in the UK for children of Caribbean descent, including West Indian, Afro-Caribbean, British Black and, more recently, African-Caribbean. In Canada the most widely used term would appear to be West Indian.

Sometimes the same terms have different connotations in the two countries. In Canada, for instance, children entering the school system unable to speak English are usually referred to as ESL students. In Britain, most teachers talk in terms of 'bilingual' rather than 'ESL' pupils, thereby stressing children's accomplishments rather than their lack of fluency in English. In Canada, however, bilingualism is more commonly associated with the French–English bilingualism which is the cornerstone of multicultural policy, rather than the Panjabi–English bilingualism of children in Ontario schools or the Cantonese–French bilingualism of children in Québec. Canadians make extensive use of 'visible minorities', a term easily understood but hardly ever used by British writers. In contrast, 'Black' is used very frequently in British academic writing and more general discussions as an umbrella term for all non-Whites, and in preference to either 'visible' or 'ethnic minorities'.

These differences sometimes cause difficulties in deciding which terminology to use in a comparative account targeted at an international audience. The solution we have adopted, wherever possible, is to use Canadian terms in discussions of the Canadian situation and British terms in discussions of British education.

Organisation of the Book

Our aim is to provide a comparative account of educational responses to multilingualism in Britain and in Canada. In order to set the scene we look in Chapter 2 at responses to diversity: what are the longstanding attitudes to other languages and culture which conditioned early responses to immigrants and how did these attitudes change over time? In particular, how did the education systems adapt to new populations and to what extent have ethnic minority children been able to fulfil their potential?

We look in Chapter 3 at the teaching of English as a second language. Traditionally, the main obstacle to educational success was perceived to be the lack of English. The priority was therefore to teach English as rapidly as possible and the children's home languages were seen to have no part to play in this process. English language teaching has, of course, undergone a considerable evolution in Canada and in the UK, with a move towards the dismantling of segregated classes and the devolution of responsibility for second language learners from specialist teachers to class and subject teachers. However, the extent to which this process has been achieved, and the level of resourcing made available for its implementation, remain a subject of concern.

A chapter on 'Diversity in the Classroom' examines the dangers of tokenism or 'celebratory multiculturalism' and looks at the wide variety of ways in which aspects of other languages and cultures can be incorporated into normal classroom practice in ways which support the cultural identity and existing language skills of ethnic minority children, while at the same time increasing the awareness of White children. It also addresses the centrality of community involvement in school in the definition of children's learning needs and priorities.

Chapter 5 looks at the question of community/heritage language teaching in Britain and in Canada. While English (and, to a lesser extent, French) have, until relatively recently, been the sole priority of mainstream educators, the transmission and maintenance of minority languages has now appeared very firmly on the educational agenda. We look at the different models of delivery in Canada and the UK and identify the strengths and weaknesses of each approach.

Finally in Chapter 6, having attempted to outline the main features of an educational programme which serves the best interests of all children, we focus on the conditions which will be necessary if the political rhetoric is to become an educational reality: before meaningful changes can take place, there must be evidence of the political will to commit resources on a far larger scale than has previously been the case.

2 Responses to Diversity

In order to evaluate current educational developments, it is important to provide a broader context for discussion. In the present chapter we will be exploring three main themes. We consider first traditional responses to diversity and the climate of opinion which this created in the early days of immigration. In both Canada and Britain, the dominant political and economic group has shown a high degree of intolerance towards diversity through social and educational policy. This history has clear implications for the way in which immigrants in the post-war period were received. Next we look specifically at the creation of diversity in Canada and the UK in the post-war years. Although there have been important differences in the immigration policies of the two countries, the social outcomes are remarkably similar, with evidence of social and ethnic stratification, particularly in areas such as employment. Finally, we look at the ways in which this stratification has manifested itself in education. We review the widespread evidence of the underachievement of ethnic minority students and examine assessment procedures which have played an important role in discriminating between different groups of children. We also look at the different phases which have emerged in educational responses to diversity over the years.

Traditional Responses to Diversity

The reactions of receiving societies to newcomers depend very much on their history. In the case of Britain and of Canada, we are dealing with societies dominated by a particular ethno-cultural group. Although multiculturalism and multilingualism have always been a fact of life, both countries have nurtured the myth of cultural and linguistic homogeneity as a means of ensuring that power stays with the dominant group. Linguistic and cultural diversity have, wherever possible, been made invisible. It is important, therefore, to understand the widespread attitudes towards linguistic and cultural diversity which existed in Canada and Britain prior to the important demographic changes which have taken place in the second half of the twentieth century.

The British history of intolerance

The British Isles, for instance, have long been marked by a diversity of traditions. The influence of the Celts, the Romans, Vikings, the Angles and Saxons and the Normans is still to be found in place names and other aspects of present-day English, the study of which offers a panorama on the past. The emergence of one social group with a stronghold on political power, however, ensured that the language and culture associated with this group enjoyed the same high status. The East Midlands dialect spoken by rich merchants in the triangle enclosed by Oxford, Cambridge and London, was promoted to the detriment of all other English dialects. This downgrading of dialects still continued hundreds of years later in schools throughout the land. In the first half of the twentieth century, it was still common for departures from East Midlands speech, now codified as standard English, to be labelled as 'sloppy', 'ungrammatical' and 'disfigured'. The task of education was to eradicate such 'vulgarisms' and replace them with what was promoted as the more elegant and expressive standard language.

If dialect speakers fared ill, the fate of speakers of languages other than English was even worse. The gradual imposition of English has been a story of power and resistance. Political and economic forces began to make inroads on the Celtic languages as early as the eleventh century, although nineteenth and twentieth-century phenomena such as industrialisation and economic restructuring considerably accelerated the process. The fact that small but significant minorities of Welsh and Scots and Irish Gaelic speakers continue against all odds to assert their rights to use their mother tongues is a powerful reminder of the potent symbolism of language in ethnic identity.

Within the education system, however, the policy was to replace the language of the home with standard English. The 1847 Report of the Church Commissioners on schools in Wales, for instance, viciously attacked the Welsh language on the grounds that it isolated 'the masses' from the 'upper portions of society', and kept them 'under hatches'. In the classroom there were cruel attempts to humiliate Welsh speakers by making anyone heard using the language wear a halter known as the 'Welsh not'. The humiliation of having to wear the halter was compounded by the pressure to 'grass' on classmates, since the last person wearing the not at the end of the day was subjected to corporal punishment. Draconian attitudes towards Celtic languages were still in evidence throughout the first half of the twentieth century.

Anglo-conformity in Canada

Canadian history resonates with a similar Anglocentric – or to be more accurate – Anglo-Celtic fervour. The rights of native Canadians have consistently been abused or made invisible by more recently arrived immigrants. Until the 1980s, native Canadian children who were sent away to school and separated from their families for years were left in no doubt that their language, culture and religion had no part to play in the modern world (York, 1989). The current state of native languages is a symptom of the vigorous attempts to assimilate aboriginal peoples. Almost all Indians now speak English and, of the 53 indigenous languages, only Inukitut, Ojibway and Cree are considered likely to survive (Foster, 1982). Certain religious groups, including the United Church of Canada and some Catholics, have formally apologised to Indian people for the social disintegration which mainstream policies have produced. Apologies, however, do nothing to change the high levels of unemployment, suicide and disease, the alcoholism and poor material conditions experienced by native peoples.

Other groups have also been subjected to assimilationist pressures. Following the defeat by the English on the Plains of Abraham, the French, French language and French culture were marginalised by the dominant English-speaking Anglo-Celts. Attempts to develop policies that accommodate French and English language needs date back to the eighteenth century (Cartwright, 1988). But while efforts to protect French have proved effective at a federal level, there has been little political support for this position outside of Québec and New Brunswick. Long standing tensions have recently re-surfaced with the failure of various provinces to ratify the Meech Lake Accord, which sought to offer Québec recognition as a 'distinct society' within Canada (see Edwards, 1992 for an analysis of events surrounding this constitutional crisis).

Even so, Francophones have resisted pressures to assimilate more successfully than other less numerous minorities. Gaelic-speaking Scots in Cape Breton, for instance, were physically punished for using the language of the home (Black, 1913; Shaw, 1983). A similar contempt has been shown for Black Canadians in Ontario who, for many years, were educated in segregated schools.

The Creation of Post-War Diversity

Canada and Britain have seen enormous demographic changes in the post- war period. In both cases, these changes were motivated by the need for economic growth. The ways in which this was achieved, however, differed in important ways between the two countries. The British solution was to turn to the Commonwealth and, in particular, to the so-called 'New Commonwealth' countries of India, Pakistan and the West Indies. Here high unemployment and pressures on the land ensured a ready supply of cheap labour to meet the demands of the post-war boom economy. Other factors also came into play. For instance, at just the point that Britain was seeking to recruit workers from the Caribbean, there was a significant tightening of control on immigration to the USA, the traditional destination for West Indian emigrants.

Newcomers were inevitably attracted to large urban centres where the work was most plentiful and to run-down inner city areas where housing was cheapest. Thus although the proportion of immigrants in the UK as a whole was very low, in some cities and in some areas of these cities, the concentration of newcomers was considerably higher.

Increasingly stringent immigration legislation enacted through the 1960s had the effect of first accelerating the rate of new arrivals in an attempt to beat the new laws and later reducing immigration to a mere trickle. By the early 1970s, the net outflow of immigrants returning to their home countries was in fact greater than the number of new settlers. From the 1970s and 1980s the largest group of immigrants were political refugees, most notably East African Asians, Vietnamese, Sri Lankan Tamils, Somalis and Eritreans. The racist nature of immigration legislation has often been the object of critical comment (see, for example, Dummett & Martin, 1982; Massey, 1991).

Immigration has been a fact of life in Britain for hundreds of years. For most of this time, however, the vast majority of settlers were of Jewish or European origin. The presence of large numbers of Black immigrants is a much more recent phenomenon. In 1951, 0.25% of the population were non-White; thirty years later, this proportion had risen to 4.7% . The failure of official British censuses to collect data on either language background or ethnicity makes it very difficult to estimate the current extent of cultural and linguistic diversity. However, the biennial Inner London Education Authority language censuses conducted throughout the 1980s give some indication. ILEA (1987) for instance, reported that 172 different languages were spoken in London schools.

The material realities for ethnic minority populations in Britain have been encapsulated in a whole series of reports but, most notably the three surveys published by the Policy Studies Institute (PSI) (Daniel, 1968; Smith, 1977; Brown, 1984). These PSI reports have shown consistently that Black workers are concentrated in unskilled and semi-skilled work; that there are substantial differences between the median weekly wages of indigenous and immigrant groups; and that promotion opportunities are far more limited for Black workers. Whereas unemployment was not an issue in the 1960s, it became a focus for increasing concern from the 1970s onwards, particularly in the Black community where a disproportionately high number of adults have not been able to find work. Brown (1984), for instance, suggests that one-and-a-half times as many Blacks as Whites are registered as unemployed. This trend is particularly marked for males over the age of 35 who live outside Inner London, Birmingham and Manchester, for whom the rates of unemployment are between twice and three times higher than for the White population. Attacks on Asians have been shown to be 50 times higher than those on White people and 36 times higher than those on West Indians (HMSO, 1981). Attention has also been focused on racial harassment in schools in the Commission for Racial Equality's (1988) report on *Learning in Terror*.

Significantly, Black people have consistently challenged mainstream racism and have played a critical role in effecting change. Strong challenges to conventional wisdom have been launched by Black academics (see, for instance, Coard, 1971; Stone, 1981; Carby, 1980; Centre for Contemporary Cultural Studies, 1982; Mullard, 1982; Brandt, 1986; Solomon, 1988; 1989). Anger about the treatment of Black people is a recurring theme in a growing body of literature as, too, is pride in Black people's achievements (L.K. Johnson, 1981; D. Johnson, 1984) Communities have organised to campaign for their home languages to be given recognition (LMP, 1985; Bourne, 1989; Cummins & Danesi, 1990). Attention has also been paid to the unacceptably low status and limited promotion prospects of Black teachers (Hubah, 1984).

The Canadian mosaic

The situation in Canada is rather different. There has been a long tradition of preference for Anglo-Celtic and Northern European immigration, although small numbers of other groups were admitted for specific kinds of work. In the nineteenth century, this vigorous 'whites only' policy even resulted in the imposition of a head tax on Chinese immigrants. From 1967, however, the Canadian government overturned all racial and ethnic criteria and implemented a point system based on factors such as education, occupational demand, age, knowledge of English and French, presence of relatives and destination within the country. Thus while the Canadian policy is highly selective it is no longer informed by inherently racist assumptions.

The legacy of racist policies, however, has undoubtedly made its mark. Porter (1965), for instance, draws attention to the over-representation of northern European Whites (but not French and Italians) in the upper levels of the occupational structure. Kalbach (1979) and Samuda (1986) point to a similar pattern whereby Anglo-Celts and other northern Europeans retain economic and political power, while Ukrainians, Italians and other European minorities occupy a middle stratum and visible minorities and native peoples remain at the bottom of the hierarchy.

At the beginning of the century, the British made up 57% of the population, the French 31% and 'others' 12%. By 1981, there had been important changes. The proportion of British and French had diminished to 40% and 27% respectively, while others had increased to 27%. The remaining 6% were of mixed ethnicity and, of these, almost three quarters had no French or British links. The diminishing influence in the post-war period of the so-called 'charter nations', and particularly of the Anglo-Celts, created what some commentators (e.g. Troper, 1979; Cummins & Troper, 1985) have described as a crisis for Canadians anxious to establish a separate identity from Americans. Multiculturalism has formed an important element in this new identity. While Americans coined the metaphor of the 'melting pot' for their own experiences of diversity, Canadians have preferred to promote the notion of a cultural mosaic. Much ink has been used in drawing attention to the shaky foundations which underpin this cultural mosaic. Writers such as Hughes & Kallen (1974), Burnet (1984), Samuda (1986), Friesen (1987) and Cummins & Danesi (1990), all point to the continuing Anglo-conformity which runs through most aspects of Canadian life.

The most popular destination for 'new Canadians' has been Ontario and, each year, between a half and two thirds of immigrants to Ontario have made their home in Metropolitan Toronto. It is therefore not surprising to find great variation in attitudes towards diversity both across Canada and within Ontario (Edwards, 1992). None the less, significant policy developments have been taking place both in relation to new ethnic minority communities and in relation to the long-standing tensions between English and French-speaking Canada.

The rise of nationalism in Québec led the federal government to set up a Royal Commission on Bilingualism and Biculturalism in the early 1960s. This drew attention to the need for Canada to develop on the basis of an equal partnership between the two founding nations; it also emphasised the importance of safeguarding the contribution of other ethnic groups to the enrichment of the nation, though it was made clear that this should not happen at the expense of either English or French (Royal Commission, 1966; 1970). In 1971, Pierre Trudeau launched a policy of 'multiculturalism within a bilingual framework', in which both French and English were to be considered official languages, but no culture and no ethnic group would take precedence over any other.

As attempts were made in the course of the 1970s to translate this policy into practice, its weaknesses gradually became clear. There have been many criticisms of the policy, including the danger that multiculturalism would sustain rather than diminish ethnic stratification (Porter, 1972; 1979; Breton, Reitz & Valentine, 1980). It has also been noted that not all minority groups are equally enthusiatsic about muliculturalism (Moghaddam & Taylor, 1987). Some arguments were aimed specifically at the notion of 'multiculturalism within a bilingual framework'. Various ethnocultural groups proposed that the notion of culture without language was unworkable and that multiculturalism would necessarily involve some form of multilingualism. Many Francophone and Anglophone Canadians feared that this development would threaten the position of French and English and create further divisions in society, an outcome hardly consistent with a policy of multiculturalism (cf. Lupul, 1981; Cummins & Danesi, 1990).

The Canadian government has had to face a very basic dilemma. The large majority of ethnic minority members consulted as part of a national survey of non-official languages (O'Bryan, Reitz & Kuplowska, 1976) supported the notion of linguistic and cultural maintenance for their children and wanted public institutional support to achieve this aim. However, a survey of ethnic majority attitudes (Berry, Kalin & Taylor, 1977) showed more limited support for cultural diversity. Whereas most Anglophones and Francophones took no exception to the celebration of minority festivals or community events, their views were considerably more guarded on the question of linguistic diversity, whether in the form of heritage language teaching in schools or minority language broadcasts.

Federal government has continued its support for minority languages throughout the 1980s, often in the face of very heated opposition. The 'Charter of Rights and Freedoms' which forms part of the new Canadian Constitution of 1982, sets out, among other things, to preserve the country's multicultural heritage and protect the right to use a range of other languages. The 1988 Multiculturalism Act also endorses this position, directing all federal institutions to make use, as appropriate, of the linguistic skills and cultural understandings of all its peoples. Its commitment to promoting multiculturalism as a fundamental feature of Canadian identity and heritage was translated into a budget of $200 million to be spent over a five year period on areas such as heritage language teaching, cross-cultural communication and race relations. The extent to which the federal policy is translated into positive practice either at provincial level or at the level of local school boards continues to be a subject of some concern (Cummins & Danesi, 1990).

The 1988 Multiculturalism Act has attracted similar criticisms to the 1971 policy of multiculturalism (Edwards, 1992). It has been argued, for instance, that the Act is politically opportunistic and socially divisive. Opposition was also expressed from within Québec by individuals who construed multiculturalism as an attempt to reduce their status to that of one minority group among many (Cummins & Danesi, 1990). The tensions have been particularly apparent in Montreal where, in the late 1980s, 82% of the students on the island had been born outside Canada. The general malaise clearly surfaced in a 1989 survey of parents and students conducted by the Montreal Catholic School Commission. One question asked specifically whether some schools should be for 'pure Québecois' and others for 'ethnics', whether they should be mixed half and half, or whether things should remain as they were (Picard, 1989). The outrage provoked by this question, particularly among the so-called allophone communities subsequently caused it to be withdrawn. The fact remains, however, that the school commissioners voted 15 to 4 in favour of its inclusion and that many Québecois are moving to the suburbs to escape the multi-ethnic realities of the city, a phenomenon which Bissonnette (1989) labels the 'British syndrome'.

Some observers have commented that the support for multiculturalism has been of a largely passive nature. Breton (1986), for instance, argues that policy developments have been given momentum by ethnic organisational elites, government agencies and political authorities rather than 'ordinary Canadians'. Edwards (1992) sums up this situation thus:

> The Canadian population has a certain (unspecified, perhaps unspecifiable) level of tolerance for diversity, a certain fund of passive goodwill, a certain willingness to see the 'others' shape their lives as desired; it does not appear to have any great sympathy for real changes in social institutions, for direct (especially financial) government involvement in ethnocultural affairs, for any substantial alteration to an Anglo-conformity pattern. In these respects it is, perhaps, like many other societies.

The Educational Response

Any developments within education need to be seen within this wider social context. It is also important to chart the relevant background issues within education itself. Awareness of the extent of underperformance has been slow in both Canada and Britain. Even when educational statistics have confirmed that ethnic minority children are not fulfilling their potential, efforts to identify the structural and attitudinal factors which discriminate between different groups of students have often been disappointing. Such efforts can only be understood, however, in the context of the different phases in the thinking which has informed school responses to diversity. In the section which follows we look at the evidence of underperformance; the role which culturally biased assessment procedures play in this underperformance; and the evolution of different educational philosophies for dealing with diversity.

Patterns of underperformance

The position of Black children in education is equally depressing. Although parental aspirations and support for children have always been high (cf. Tomlinson, 1984; Brah & Minhas, 1988), the ability or willingness of British schools to help ethnic minority children to achieve their potential has been seriously questioned. Schools in the inner city areas where immigrants settled were already poorly resourced and under pressure in the 1950s and 1960s (Plowden, 1967) and were not at all equipped to respond effectively to large numbers of new children arriving throughout the school year.

These conditions produced a national picture first officially recognised in the Statistics of Education (DES, 1970), in which disproportionately low numbers of ethnic minority children were to be found in selective schools, higher streams and examination classes. Different ethnic groups, however, were performing at different levels. There appeared to be a hierarchical situation whereby non-immigrants did better than immigrants, and all immigrants did better than West Indians. The figures which produced the greatest protest, however, were those which revealed the over-representation of West Indian children in schools for the educationally subnormal. On a national level there were proportionately four times as many West Indian children in ESN schools as indigenous children, and in Greater London these figures were higher still. As the extent of wrongful placement became more widely known (publicised, for instance, by the highly influential pamphlet by Coard (1971), *How the West Indian Child is Made Educationally Sub-Normal in the British School System*), the ESN issue became the rallying point for much broader anxiety and disquiet with the educational performance of Black children.

Current patterns of performance are extremely difficult to discern, though the indications are that many ethnic minority children continue to underachieve. Tomlinson (1986), for instance, in a review of research on underachievement, suggests that Asians perform as well as Whites and that both achieve higher than West Indians. Massey (1991), however, points to evidence that Asians achieve as well as Whites only because they stay in education longer; and also to the fact that some Asians, notably Bangladeshis, do not perform as well as Whites.

Studies conducted in the 1980s have helped produce a clearer picture of the processes and structures which perpetuate inequality. Cashmore (1982) and Leaman & Carrington (1985), for instance, point to the ways in which Black children are channelled from academic pursuits into sport, while various other in-depth studies (Fuller, 1983; Wright, 1986) indicate that pupils are not achieving their full potential because of teacher racism and institutional racism.

Studies of school effectiveness have introduced another dimension to the debate. The ORACLE studies of primary and secondary education (Galton *et al.*, 1980; Delamont and Galton, 1986), the (1984) Hargreaves Report on comprehensive schools within the Inner London Education Authority and the (1985) Fish Report on children with special educational needs all stress the importance of 'whole school' approaches to learning. Smith & Tomlinson (1989) also explore this notion in an in-depth study of selected comprehensive schools. They found, for instance, that ethnic minority children of comparable measured potential at age 11 achieve considerably better qualifications when they attend 'effective' schools. Much more research, however, needs to be done on what constitutes good practice in such 'effective' schools.

Underperformance of ethnic minority students would also seem to be a problem in the Candian context. Interestingly, Canadian studies of educational performance and ethnicity in the late 1960s (Wright, 1971) and mid-1970s (Deosoran, 1976) showed a high overall level of attainment for minority students. However, later studies, together with the informal observations of teachers, suggest that students from *some* minority groups are seriously underperforming. Cummins (1984) shows how a sample of 400 children from non-English-speaking homes achieved significantly lower scores than their English-speaking peers on the Wechsler Intelligence Scale for Children – Revised (WISC-R), the most commonly used IQ test in Canadian schools. He also points to similar patterns of underperformance in Metropolitan Toronto schools. Wright & Tsuji (1984), for instance, document the over-representation of certain minority group students in vocational programmes for secondary students in a number of Metropolitan Toronto boards of education.

Some attention has also been paid to the processes which mediate underperformance. Thus, Solomon (1988; 1989) shows how Black children in Canada, as in Britain, disengage from the academic curriculum to pursue an alternative reward structure: the sports sub-culture. Black students may therefore choose to stay in school but be seriously under-represented in academic programmes. In a similar vein, Samuda (1986) argues that inappropriate placement and counselling of students act as serious blocks to equal opportunites in Canada.

Assessment

The processes which mediate different levels of achievement for different ethnic groups are clearly highly complex. For the present purposes, however, we will focus on the critical role of assessment, a subject which has received a great deal of attention in both Canada and Britain. Although standardised testing is markedly less important in British than in North American education, this form of assessment is none the less in widespread use. For instance, all primary schools in the sample examined by the Evaluation of Testing in Schools Project (1980-84) made use of standardised tests, particularly for the assessment of reading ability at 7 plus. In the secondary sector, 75% of schools used standardised tests. However, over half of these schools tested only one age group, year 7 children (11 years of age), as they transferred from primary to secondary school.

A wide range of criticisms has been made against standardised testing in many different countries (cf. Brière, 1973; Stenhouse, 1975; Cummins, 1984; Laycock, 1989; Gipps et al., 1983; Hodges, 1990). Such tests are based on an outdated and oversimplified view of the learning process. They yield little information on children's progress over time nor, in most cases, do they throw light on how a child is going about a particular task, information which is essential if the teacher is to respond effectively to the needs of the individual. There are also anxieties about the consistency of test results with the same child achieving very different scores on different standardised tests.

Standardised testing poses difficulties for all children but is particularly problematic in relation to ethnic minority children. There is now a widespread understanding that most standardised tests are culturally biased for any group which does not come from the same socio-cultural background as the group used as the basis for standardising the test (Hegarty & Lucas, 1978). The reference group in Britain and North America is invariably White, middle-class and English-speaking and differs in important respects from many of the other social class and ethnic groups which make up the population. The kinds of problems created for minority students by this cultural bias are neatly illustrated by items selected by Cummins & Bountrogianni (1986) from the WISC-R intelligence test widely used in Canadian schools. Questions such as 'How many pennies in a nickel?' 'Who discovered America? and 'How tall is the average

Canadian man?' will inevitably pose difficulties for students from minority backgrounds whose experience is unlikely to have brought them into contact with information of this kind.

In British schools, other forms of assessment have also attracted criticism, including the half-yearly examinations in secondary schools which are often used as the basis for changing children between groups, and styles of response to children's work which stress the negative rather than positive achievements (cf. Chatwin, 1990). Dissatisfaction with existing practice has led to a number of important developments in assessment procedures. For instance, there has been a move, notably in General Certificate of Secondary Education (GCSE) exams, towards continuous assessment which gives a picture of children's progress over time. There is also a growing reliance on multi-faceted approaches which feed into a more comprehensive picture of children's achievements. Often this has entailed teachers *describing* performance rather than attempting to *measure* it. The emphasis, increasingly, has been on 'formative' approaches which seek information to guide teaching, a development which potentially enhances the professional role of the teacher. In parallel, there has been a move towards criterion referencing (see, for instance, Barrs *et al.*, 1988; 1990) which focuses on what a child can actually do, and a move away from norm referencing which sets out what a child of a given age *should* be able to do.

The Education Reform Act (ERA) (1988) introduced a new dimension to the debate on assessment. It imposed a National Curriculum for state schools consisting of three core subjects and seven foundation subjects for 5-16 year old children. It also made provision for the testing of children at 7, 11, 14 and 16 and for the publication of school results. Underlying these reforms, and other aspects or ERA, was the faith that 'market forces' would improve educational standards. The introduction of National Curriculum assessment has predictably given rise to a great deal of concern in an education system where considerable agnosticism regarding the value of standardised tests was already widespread. Gipps (1990), for instance, has pointed to the ways in which tests will undermine a supportive classroom ethos by fostering competition and a fear of failure. Anxieties have also been expressed about the ways in which testing downgrades the role of the teacher by undervaluing informed professional judgement (Chatwin, 1990).

Government policy was based on the minimum competency testing familiar to North American educators which requires teachers to administer and mark a centrally-set test (Gram, 1988; Surkes, 1989). The Task Group on Assessment and Testing (DES, 1988c), however, raised a number of objections to this form of assessment, reflecting the changing attitudes towards assessment which had been gaining ground in many schools. The proposed modifications attempt to reconcile the conflicting demands of politicians and professionals, but have already been criticised as unwieldy and unworkable. Debate on these matters continues and is by no means resolved at the time of writing.

In the UK, the debate on assessment which has followed in the wake of the Education Reform Act has also focused, to some extent at least, on the ways in which the new test procedures will put second language learners at a particular disadvantage. The Task Group on Testing and Assessment (DES, 1988c) suggested that children in the early stages of learning English might be exempted from tests. No guidance is offered, however, on what criteria should be used in assessing children's competence in English in order to arrive at a decision as to whether or not they should be exempted. The Task Group also advocated that assessment in skills other than English should be conducted in the pupil's first language 'wherever practicable and necessary'. Two years later, however, the National Curriculum Assessment Arrangements (DES, 1990b) took a rather different stance. They argued that the translation of Standardised Assessment Tasks (SATs) into pupils' home languages was unrealistic, because of the range of languages spoken in schools, and undesirable because of the need for 'quality control'. They demonstrate a similarly narrow understanding of the situation of bilingual children in their advice that teachers should not accept pupils' responses in their home language as evidence of attainment in English. In this view, testing is concerned only with productive and not with receptive abilities.

There is a widespread feeling that policy on assessment is ill-formulated and ethnocentric and that, where reference is made to minority pupils, this is done very much as an afterthought and with limited understanding of the wider implications. Little thought seems to have been given, for instance, to the changes in teaching styles which are likely to result from the new regime. The requirement for schools to publish test results will inevitably produce pressures for teachers to 'teach to the test' in order to improve the children's scores. The move in recent years has been away from a transmission model of teaching in which the pupil plays a largely passive role to methods which encourage children to be active participants in the learning process. Such techniques have proved particularly effective in allowing second language learners access to the full curriculum (for further discussion, see Chapter 4) and a return to more traditional methods cannot be in their best interests.

It should be acknowledged, however, that the assessment procedures associated with the National Curriculum *do* have some potential value in the debate on educational equality. Early informal reports indicate that teacher estimates of ethnic minority achievement are often considerably below their actual scores on the SATS. This information is clearly valuable in raising the issue of low expectations with teachers. In addition, testing of this kind offers opportunities both for ethnic monitoring in the widest sense and for examining the effectiveness of particular teaching strategies with minority pupils. It would be possible, for instance, to compare the performance of children receiving bilingual support (see Chapter 4) with those who had been taught solely through the medium of English.

Assessment in Canadian schools

Despite the extensive research undertaken throughout the 1970s and 1980s in the USA on the discriminatory nature of the assessment of minority students, discussion of these issues in Canada, either on an academic level or in the formulation of education legislation, has been minimal (Cummins, 1988). Where discussion has taken place, the focus has been almost exclusively on the inappropriateness of standardised testing procedures for speakers of English as a second language. Cummins (1984) for instance, points to the fact that, whereas children acquire native-like conversational skills within two years of exposure to the new language, it can take up to five years to develop academic aspects of language proficiency. It follows that children who have acquired conversational fluency cannot automatically be assumed to be able to perform on a par with native speakers on academic tasks. Psychological tests performed within the first five years thus risk underestimating minority students' potential.

Awareness of the need to guard against biased assessment exists at both federal and provincial levels. The federal report, *Equality Now* (House of Commons, 1984), for instance, acknowledges the need for research on assessment procedures used to place students in occupational and academic streams in schools. In a similar vein, the Ontario Ministry of Education advises that assessment should either take place in the child's first language or be postponed. However, while there may be some sensitivity to these issues at federal and provincial levels, the picture on the ground has been less encouraging. Samuda & Crawford (1980) report that very few school boards in Ontario had developed policies on the placement and assessment of children for whom English was not the first language. They also suggest that, even in boards with a written policy, those responsible for educational assessment often failed to act in accordance with the policy. Cummins (1988: 146) comments on the general situation thus:

It is disturbing to contrast the concern for issues of discriminatory assessment in the United States with the virtual absence of any sustained consideration of these issues in Ontario, with the exception of a few boards of education. One might have expected the endorsement of multicultural education policies in Ontario would make policy makers and psychologists highly sensitive to issues of educational equity but there is little evidence that this has been the case.

Fortunately, there is some evidence that the level of awareness of problems associated with assessment increased significantly through the 1980s. Cummins & Bountrogianni (1986), for instance, report that, in many school systems, practitioners are actively attempting to come to grips with the issues. And Cummins (1988) refers, in passing, to the 'multicultural assessment system' of the North York Board of Education which forms part of Metropolitan Toronto.

It was certainly our experience in the Ferndale Board that attitudes towards standardised testing for second language learners were extremely cautious and heavy emphasis was placed on teacher observation. A supervisory officer explained practice in the following terms:

> If there's a concern about a child's lack of development after a period of time, the ESL consultant might get involved, but it's up to the teacher to observe, to record, to modify the program and see what impact that has before it goes to the next step.

In summary, assessment has been and will almost certainly continue to be a contentious issue, partly because it places certain groups of children at a disadvantage and partly because of the disagreement over the way in which it should be undertaken. The presence of children from different cultural and linguistic backgrounds in the schools of Canada and the UK brings such issues to the fore. Many constructive ways forward have been identified. Traditional assumptions about the role of standardised testing, however, are a formidable obstacle to more flexible and responsive alternatives.

Changing paradigms

There have been a number of distinct phases in the responses of educationalists to linguistic and cultural diversity. In a British context, Massey (1991) for instance, identifies six different stages which he describes as overlapping rather than distinct. Initially, the response was one of inaction or 'laissez-faire'. The assumption was that immigrants would be absorbed with little difficulty into what essentially was a tolerant society. Rapidly, however, racial tension boiled over into public disturbances and required a rather different response. The solution was seen to lie in the *assimilation* of immigrants through tighter controls on the number of new arrivals. In an educational context, the Department of Education and Science (DES) gave permission to Local Education Authorities to bus immigrant children to other schools when the proportion of immigrants reached 33%. A more subtle approach to assimilation emerged in the mid-1960s in the form of *integration* through compensation. The different linguistic and cultural backgrounds of immigrant children were seen within a pathological framework: schools and teachers needed to help them conform to British expectations if they were to succeed in British society.

During the 1970s there was a distinct move from notions of compensatory education to *cultural pluralism* as multicultural education established itself in schools. Underlining this approach was the assumption that the underachievement and alienation of Black children could be improved by increasing their self-esteem through showing respect for minority cultures in the school curriculum. Multiculturalism has been criticised on the grounds that it is often tokenistic and fails to engage with the racism which is part of every day reality for large numbers of Black people (see, for example, Stone, 1981, Mullard, 1982, and the Centre for Contemporary Cultural Studies, 1982). None the less, multicultural education was widely regarded as a route to greater social cohesion and, by the late 1970s, local education authorities such as the ILEA and Manchester began to develop specific policies in response to the presence of ethnic minority children in schools.

Anti-racist approaches have attempted to answer the criticisms of multiculturalism by identifying examples of racism in school practices and curriculum materials. Whereas multicultural education tended to be aimed at ethnic minority children in inner city schools, anti-racism is considered to be of concern to all children, irrespective of ethnicity. Early LEA policies had concentrated on inter-cultural understanding; later policy development, however, has dealt directly with issues of equality and social justice (cf. Troyna & Williams, 1986; Massey, 1991). During the course of the 1980s there were increasing moves to synthesise anti-racism and multicultural education into *anti-racist multiculturalism*, with writers such as Grinter (1985) and Craft & Klein (1986) arguing that both approaches are necessary if any real progress is to be made.

Developments in anti-racist education have been the object of a considerable right wing backlash in the UK (see, e.g. Flew, 1987; Lewis, 1988). Allegations have been made, for instance, that the politicisation of the curriculum and the failure to transmit a common British culture has been responsible for falling standards in British school. Such assertions are patently based on a distrust and fear of cultural pluralism *per se*; they also rely on hearsay rather than research. A similar disquiet with the principles of anti-racist education can also be perceived in two recent developments—the new criteria for the administration of Section 11 of the 1966 Local Government Act, and the 1988 Education Reform Act.

Section 11 monies were originally targeted at partially funding posts which would be of direct benefit to New Commonwealth communities. In the early days, the vast majority of such posts had been used for the teaching of English as a Second Language. Increasingly, however, Section 11 had been used for multicultural and anti-racist initiatives of benefit to *all* children. Under the new criteria, this source of funding can only be used for teaching of English as a second language and strengthening ties between schools and minority parents, a development which is being interpreted as a reassertion of an assimilationist agenda (Hatcher, 1990). The 1988 Education Reform Act (ERA), also shows signs of resistance to anti-racism. Great concern has been expressed about the ethnocentric assumptions of National Curriculum English (cf. Bourne & Cameron, 1988; Stubbs, 1989) and History and Religious Education (Massey, 1991).

The present discussion has been based very firmly on developments within British education. There is evidence, however, of a very similar pattern of development in Canadian education. Descriptions of assimilationist policies are common (see, for instance, Cummins & Danesi, 1990). However, accounts of multicultural education are now beginning to appear (cf. Esling, 1989); so, too, are discussions of anti-racism (Cummins, 1988). Multiculturalism and anti-racism would appear, however, to be more recent items on the educational agenda in Canada than in the UK, no doubt because of the different patterns of immigration in the two countries. It is significant that, while progress from assimilationist to anti-racist approaches has taken place on a shorter time-scale in Canada, the development in teachers' thinking has followed the same course. (For other national perspectives, see contributors to Skutnabb-Kangas & Cummins, 1988).

In discussing development in the post-war period it is easy to give the impression of linear development. The situation is, of course, a great deal more complex. It is quite clearly not the case, for instance, that teachers as a group abandoned assimilationist ideas and progressed uniformly through a multicultural phase before realising that an anti-racist dimension needed to inform a multicultural philosophy. Within most schools there is an enormous range of experience and opinions. At one end of the continuum, many teachers still subscribe to a pathological model which expects that ethnic minority children should abandon their own languages and cultures in favour of those of the dominant group. At the other end of the continuum, many teachers have perceived the dangers of tokenism and are actively addressing aspects of institutionalised racism. The vast majority of teachers in Canada and the UK, however, can almost certainly be placed at various points between these poles, expressing enormous goodwill and genuine concern for the ethnic minority children they teach, but with varying levels of perception of their own ethnocentricism, of their own low expectations or of the institutional aspects of school life which ensure that Black children do not have access to the same range of opportunities as their White peers.

E pluribus unum?

In this chapter we have examined the traditional intolerance of diversity in Canada and the UK which shaped the response to significant numbers of immigrants from many different parts of the world in the post-war period. There is no shortage of evidence in either country of what Porter (1965) first called 'the vertical mosaic', a social and ethnic stratification in which 'visible minorities' have considerably less access than Whites to economic and political power. The same patterns of discrimination found in areas like employment are repeated in the underachievement of ethnic minority children in education. Various contributory factors come into play, including assessment procedures which are better suited to the majority group than to children for whom English is a second language or dialect, and whose cultural experience is often very different. Awareness of issues such as these has tended to be slow and teachers have moved only gradually from attempts to assimilate newcomers to mainstream norms and expectations, to the celebration of differences and, more recently, to identifying school practices and curriculum materials which are discriminatory in effect, if not in intent. This background information forms a necessary starting point for the discussion of the teaching of English as a second language, the focus for chapter three, as well as for the discussion of classroom issues in chapter four and of minority language teaching in Chapter 5.

3 Teaching English as a Second Language

Both Canada and Britain have extensive experience of linguistic diversity. For instance, the needs of French speaking children in Québec or Ontario, and Ukrainian children in the prairie provinces have been on the educational agenda for some time. By the same token, there has been much discussion of the education of Welsh and Gaelic speaking children in Wales and Scotland. As we saw in the previous chapter, however, developments in the post-war period have resulted in much more heterogeneous school populations. Classes which include children from dozens of different language backgrounds have become the norm for growing numbers of schools in both countries.

For many years the learning needs of children in multilingual classes were defined exclusively in terms of access to the English language, thereby deflecting attention from many other aspects of the education system which have a direct bearing on equality of opportunity and outcome. More recently, language learning has been placed in a much broader educational and political context, resulting in a very different interpretation of the needs of ethnic minority children. In this chapter, we will look at developments in the philosophy and practice of ESL in Britain and in Canada, tracing the evolution from an essentially assimilationist approach to one informed by the imperatives of multicultural and anti-racist education.

ESL in the UK

Early responses to marked and rapid demographic changes in post-war Britain were, as we suggested in Chapter 2, assimilationist in nature. Since lack of fluency in English was an obvious obstacle to assimilation, the educational needs of immigrant children were seen almost solely in terms of the teaching of English. This preoccupation is made clear in a wide range of government and other publications of the period. The first official advice to teachers came in a Ministry of Education (1963) pamphlet, significantly entitled 'English for Immigrants'. The Schools Council (1967) 'Working

Paper on English for the Children of Immigrants' shows a similar approach to English language teaching, talking of the 'need to provide through language the means whereby the child becomes part of his community – to provide the key to cultural and social assimilation'.

Attitudes towards linguistic diversity during this period were often very negative. The work of the British sociologist, Basil Bernstein (collected in Bernstein, 1970) is interesting in this respect. Although he denies that it was ever his intention, his work was widely interpreted as suggesting that children from working class backgrounds were linguistically deprived. Such views were sometimes generalised to second language learners. Department of Education and Science (DES)(1971: 9), for instance, argues that:

> If there is any validity in Bernstein's view that the restricted code of many culturally deprived children may hinder their ability to develop certain kinds of thinking, it is certainly applicable to non-English speaking children who may be suffering, not only from the limitation of a restricted code in their own language, but from the complication of trying to learn a second language... The bilingual situation can be a very bewildering one for immigrant children and can produce within them a psychological and emotional insecurity.

Linguistic minority children were thus often placed within a pathological framework and seen as having problems which could only be resolved through intensive English teaching in isolation from the mainstream. The prevailing beliefs and practices of this period also throw light on this isolationist approach to language learning (Levine, 1990b). Throughout the history of compulsory schooling, provision had been made on the basis of both class (private versus state schools) and perceived ability (through selective versus non- selective schools and streaming). Against this background, there is a certain logic that children with little or no English should be offered separate provision.

The early organisation of ESL teaching was problematic. Newly arrived children were being admitted to inner city schools where physical conditions and resources were often far from satisfactory (Plowden, 1967), and where teachers were totally unprepared to meet the needs of children learning English. The shortage of language teachers with specialist qualifications has been an ongoing problem in UK schools for over thirty years (Townsend, 1971; Townsend & Brittan, 1972; Bakhsh & Walker, 1980; DES, 1988b). Concerns have also been voiced more recently about the exploitation and limited professional development of Black teachers of English as a Second Language (Hubah, 1984).

Most Local Education Authorities (LEAs) responded to changing circumstances by establishing separate 'language centres' where the intention
was to teach children enough English, over a period of approximately two
years, to join the mainstream. During this time, children were, as a matter
of course, separated from their English-speaking peers. Segregated provision of this kind was certainly justified in terms of the theories of language
learning which prevailed at that time. Some commentators (e.g. Reid,
1988), however, have argued that this situation served the purpose of
satisfying majority parents, concerned that the presence of large numbers
of immigrant children would hold their own children back. It is indicative
of prevailing assimilationist assumptions that there is no documentation
on whether ethnic minority parents considered separate English language
teaching adequately met their children's needs.

The most important focus within language learning during this period
was on the grammatical structures of English. A notable example of this
approach are the early SCOPE materials which grew out of a much acclaimed curriculum development project starting in the mid-1960s. Main
emphasis was placed on a structural analysis of English and the learning
of sentence patterns through drilling. There was no place at all for children's first languages in this approach and it was not uncommon for
teachers to advise parents that it was in their children's best interests for
the family to speak only English at home (Alladina & Edwards, 1990).

Multicultural education

Until the late 1960s, teachers considered the educational needs of ethnic
minority children to be exclusively linguistic. It was assumed that such
needs were merely temporary and would be met by specialist language
teaching. By the early 1970s, however, there was some recognition that the
situation was a great deal more complex. A DES (1972:1) pamphlet on 'The
Continuing Needs of Immigrants', for instance, acknowledges that 'many
children may require occasional special help throughout their school lives'.
The growing awareness of the difference between 'survival English'
necessary for basic social relations and the continued development of
English for studying school subjects gradually gave rise to a distinction
between first, second and even third stage learners.

It thus became clear over a period of time that the needs of linguistic
minority children were neither exclusively linguistic nor were they temporary. This realisation took place within a framework of changing educational responses to diversity. As we discussed in chapter two, the early
1970s saw a marked shift from approaches which attempted to 'assimilate'
ethnic minority children to a more pluralist, multicultural stance. The

exclusive focus on ESL provision as a means of meeting ethnic minority needs was gradually replaced by arguments that minority children should be encouraged to maintain and develop their own linguistic and cultural resources within the school.

This change of emphasis also had implications for West Indian children. For as long as British schools defined the educational problems of immigrants in purely linguistic terms, pupils from the Caribbean found themselves in an anomalous position. The official language of the former British West Indian territories was English. Yet the majority of children from African-Caribbean families spoke a variety quite distinct from British English which teachers and others often found extremely difficult to understand. By the time it was acknowledged that dialect differences might be associated with educational underachievement, most children were already speaking British varieties of English and special language provision was no longer appropriate (Edwards, 1986). Many children, however, have retained distinctively Black speech features as a symbol of their ethnic identity and as a way of rejecting the low status ascribed to them by mainstream White society. The move from assimilation to multiculturalism made it easier to recognise this deliberate pattern of language choice as a political statement rather than an educational problem. And, as we will see in Chapter 5, it also created opportunities for teachers to acknowledge Black language as part of the wider linguistic resources in the classroom.

The first official recognition of this change in direction came with the publication of the report of the Bullock Committee (1975), *A Language for Life*. Its recommendation that:

> No child should be expected to cast off the language and culture of the home as he crosses the school threshold and the curriculum should reflect those aspects of his life (p. 286)

placed multiculturalism firmly on the educational agenda for the rest of the 1970s and early 1980s. While it was outside the remit of the committee to examine the teaching of English as a Second Language, various recommendations had far-reaching implications for the future development of ESL provision. For instance, the report raised the issue of the isolationist nature of much teaching, arguing that it was a matter of 'common sense' that immigrant children should not be cut off from the social and educational life of the rest of the school. It also urged specialist language teachers and other subject teachers to work closely together and placed responsibility for children's language learning needs on *all* teachers. For the first time, the role of the language teacher in multiracial schools was conceived in terms of 'consultant and adviser across the curriculum rather than of teacher confined to a single room'. *A Language For Life* thus made it possible to disentangle ESL teachers from a structure where their sole responsibility was for beginners.

Moving into the mainstream

In drawing attention to the isolation of much ESL teaching, the Bullock Report was reflecting widespread teacher worries about the divisive nature of withdrawal classes, where the only native English-speaking model available to language learners was the teacher and where there was no other opportunity for interaction with fluent speakers of English (see, for example, Levine, 1990b). For many years, the first language had been seen largely as a source of interference in the learning of subsequent languages. Now second language learning was being presented as a process of building on the knowledge speakers had already acquired of the first. Many writers (e.g. Cummins, 1984; Dulay, Burt & Krashen, 1982; Levine, 1981; Wiles, 1981) began to argue that language is learned more effectively when it is used in order to communicate. There was also a growing appreciation of the ways in which other curriculum areas, such as maths and science, could support and even increase the potential for language learning.

Research findings added weight to these anxieties. Hale & Burdar (1970), for instance, showed that adolescent language learners in Hawaii who had social contact with English speakers but received no ESL specialist help progressed more rapidly than children who had no such contact but who received specialist help. An investigation of 500 elementary and high school pupils in the USA conducted by Fathman (1976) also reported that students receiving more ESL provision progressed less rapidly than those receiving less support of this nature. The inevitable conclusion from studies such as this is that ESL provision might not necessarily hasten language learning.

There was also a gradual realisation of the racist implications of this form of delivery (Chatwin, 1985; CRE, 1986), since children taught in isolation or withdrawn from the mainstream for considerable periods did not have access to a full curriculum. Teachers were beginning to suggest that *all* children – immigrant and indigenous – should be educated for life in a multicultural society. By the early 1980s, the need for an urgent reappraisal of the organisation and content of ESL teaching was becoming clear.

The move towards mainstreaming received a considerable boost with the publication of the 1985 Swann Report, *Education For All*, which came out firmly against separate provision of any kind. It recommended that the needs of bilingual learners should be met within the mainstream school as part of a comprehensive policy of language education for *all* children. It also reiterated the position of the Bullock Report that *all* teachers have a responsibility for bilingual pupils and should be given appropriate support and training to discharge this responsibility. The Swann committee thus reflected much current thinking among educationalists. It also legitimated approaches already being developed in schools.

Because of the decentralised organisation of education in the UK, the move away from segregated ESL classes in centres and in schools took place at very uneven rates from one part of the country to another. Other factors also came into play, as might be expected in a process of change which so radically challenged long-standing assumptions and practices. Levine (1990b: 25) sums up these problems in the following terms:

> An alignment between mainstream and special English teachers is no simple matter to achieve. Clearly it has been hugely complicated by the piecemeal nature of the response to it, and by varying perceptions of what it might be; not to mention that such a shift in provision was not universally welcomed by teachers on either side [i.e. mainstream and specialist teachers]

Growing dissatisfaction with the speed of change crystallised in a formal investigation of provision for teaching English as a Second Language in Calderdale LEA (CRE, 1986). Children newly arrived or recently returned from countries in the Asian sub-continent, as well as those born in the UK with home languages other than English, were required to undergo educational screening to see if they should be placed in a special language class on admission to Calderdale schools. The CRE (1986) found that this provision had been discriminatory in effect and was in breach of both education and race relations legislation. The Report also addressed issues which had previously received relatively little attention, including the time which children lost by being bussed to school, the lack of continuity in their education and reduced access to the curriculum.

One of the effects of the investigation was to accelerate the rate of closure of language centres, although this often presented serious administrative and financial problems. For instance, the schools' building programme in some LEAs had not kept up with the increasing school population, so that there was a shortage of places in mainstream schools for pupils from language centres (Bourne, 1989: 72–3). None the less, language centres had virtually disappeared by the late 1980s with the vast majority of LEAs integrating bilingual pupils into the mainstream. By now the official sanction for integrated provision was unequivocal.

The organisational structures developed to put these changes into practice are many and varied. Bourne's (1989) survey of LEA provision for bilingual pupils in 1985–87 revealed that large numbers of authorities were expanding and consolidating their English language support services. Often this was achieved by reorganising the service and recruiting more language support teachers. Many other LEAs, however, were reorganising provision without notably expanding their staff numbers. In the majority of cases, this was being achieved by increasing the numbers of advisory (consultant) posts. In still other cases, efforts were being made to change the nature of the service more radically. For instance, one LEA had merged various services such as the language, literacy and numeracy support service, the multicultural development service and the ethnic minority service into an Education Development Service where common training would allow personnel to share expertise. It is ironic that at the same time as LEAs with high proportions of ethnic minority pupils were developing structures which would allow responsibility for language development to pass from specialists to classroom teachers, at least one county with a low proportion of minority pupils was introducing specialist language teaching structures for ESL for the first time.

New pedagogies

Attempts to integrate second language learners raised a number of uncomfortable questions. Bourne (1989), for instance, has described the mainstream as 'a place of inexplicit, covert evaluation and stratification of pupils', in which certain groups underachieve disproportionately. Much of the discussion around the changes necessary for bilingual learners to benefit from integrated provision has centred on appropriate pedagogies.

There was an urgent need, for instance, for schools to reappraise both their classroom organisation and the activities which they offered children. The interests of language learners would not be well-served by transplanting them unsupported in the traditional, teacher-centred 'talk and chalk' classroom. The growing understanding of the role of talk in the learning of all children had helped many teachers to think of alternative ways of arranging their classrooms so as to maximise the opportunities for discussion in small groups and pairs. The fact remained, however, that many mainstream classrooms, particularly at the secondary level, were not organised in this way (Galton *et al.*, 1980; Mortimore *et al.*, 1988).

Various curriculum development projects attempted to provide materials and a framework for the move away from segregated provision. Towards the end of the 1970s, the first teaching materials for use in multilingual, mixed ability classrooms began to appear in LEAs with substantial numbers of ethnic minority students. The Inner London Education Authority was at the forefront of these developments. 'The Second Language Learners in the Primary School Project' (SLIPP), for instance, attempted to identify examples of strategies in the mainstream class which were helpful to bilingual children, and to explore additional ways of supporting them and their teachers. The examples of good practice identified by SLIPP were later adapted to different age ranges. In 1978, 'The Bilingual Under Fives Project' (BUF) examined the needs of very young bilinguals; while, in 1983, 'The Second Language Learners in the Mainstream Classroom Project' (SLIM) began to look at good practice in secondary schools. The pioneering work undertaken by these ILEA projects led ultimately to two further curriculum development projects funded by outside agencies – 'The Languages in the Multicultural Primary Classroom Project' and 'The Bilingual Learners in Secondary Schools Project'. The hallmark of these various projects is the opportunities which they offer for language learning through collaborative activities across the curriculum. Bourne & McPake (1991, Reading 6) summarise the main principles of this approach as follows:

- learning is often best achieved through enquiry-based activities involving discussion
- to learn a language it is necessary to participate in its meaningful use
- the curriculum itself is therefore a useful vehicle for language learning
- some curriculum subjects are structured in such a way that they themselves give support to children learning English (e.g. through the patterning of certain activities and thus of certain structures)
- one of the main strategies, then, for both curriculum learning and language learning is the flexible use of small group work.
- this way of working also allows for the development of bilingual children's other languages – when encouragement is given for their use in the curriculum, and especially if a bilingual teacher sharing the same language is also present.
- by starting from encouraging children to apply their personal and already acquired knowledge to solving group problems, and from observing their efforts in a collaborative situation, teachers can identify and provide any support that might be needed by individual children to acquire curriculum concepts and the languages needed to express them
- pupils themselves can be involved in sharing with their teachers the direction and development of their own learning

While a policy of mainstreaming has been very widely accepted at the LEA level, moves to encourage specialist teachers to work collaboratively with class or subject teachers have received a very mixed reception in schools and have given rise to considerable confusion on the part of specialist and mainstream teachers alike. Various models of collaborative teaching are to be found. The first is essentially a remedial model in which the specialist or 'support' teacher concentrates on the individual, preparing simplified worksheets, discussing a topic in withdrawal periods before it is introduced in the main class, or consolidating the work done by the whole group at a later point. This approach has been widely criticised for its failure to address the fundamental issues of appropriate classroom organisation and the shared responsibility of the mainstream teacher for language development. Riley & Bleach (1985: 77), for instance, lament the number of teachers:

> who still expect a recently arrived beginner user of English to 'fit in' with the class without any change in their teaching, without making any accommodation towards the newcomer. Wanting to help pupils in such situations, ESL teachers find themselves writing supplementary worksheets – often an impossible task and one which in the end changes nothing. With such little job satisfaction it is not surprising that work in withdrawal classes – on or off the school site – remains attractive to ESL teachers in both language centres and schools.

Bourne (1989) also points to the unfortunate messages for the hidden curriculum of such a model. Support teachers are likely to be seen as compensating for a perceived English language deficit or underachievement in certain children. Attention is therefore focused on what the children are considered to lack rather than on the range of skills and achievements which they bring with them to the classroom.

A second model of language support takes a whole curriculum approach, sometimes known as co-operative teaching, in which the support teacher is an equal partner in planning for the whole class. The specialist knowledge of the support teacher helps the mainstream teacher develop strategies which take into account the diversity of language and learning needs. The negotiation of such a relationship, however, can sometimes be extremely difficult. There have been reports of difficulties concerning the status of the support teacher which are, no doubt, exacerbated by the expectations raised by the very use of the word 'support'. The confusion which exists in many people's minds is neatly illustrated by the anecdote of the classroom teacher who introduced the support teacher to the children with, 'And this is my friend, Carol'!

The relationship between mainstream and support teachers is a complex one which deserves careful thought. Do support and mainstream teacher have responsibility for both monolingual and bilingual pupils? What are the preferences of the individual teacher for teaching style? Who is responsible for marking, assessing pupils' needs and discipline? What arrangements can be made for joint planning of lessons? How is the subject to be presented? Without an agreed policy on issues of this kind, support teachers are often left standing for long periods on the sidelines while the class teacher addresses children. They may find themselves helping children with tasks that they feel have little educational value. Alternatively, they may find that they have nothing to do while children are involved in undemanding tasks which offer little scope for teacher intervention (Hart, 1986).

More recently, attempts have been made to develop a model of 'partnership teaching' which builds on and extends the notion of co-operative teaching by linking the work of the two teachers in the classroom with policy developments in the school as a whole. An in-service pack consisting of three videos and extensive back-up materials has been developed by the National Foundation for Educational Research in conjunction with the DES (Bourne & McPake, 1991) The authors of the pack describe this new approach in the following terms:

> The emphasis is on reviewing practice, setting short-term goals. 'experimenting' (teacher action-research) evaluating joint work and disseminating the results to the rest of the school (and sometimes across other schools). It includes teachers working together *outside* as well as inside the classroom, to make the curriculum responsive to the language needs of all pupils (p. 13).

The DES offered free training sessions for a limited period during 1990–91 to all LEAs, aimed at advisers, inspectors, head teachers and senior management as well as Section 11 teachers. The aim was thus to 'train the trainers'. At the time of writing the uptake of this offer has been encouraging and the response to the materials favourable. The long term future of partnership teaching, however, remains to be seen. While the development of the in-service materials is an extremely welcome first step, it is unclear whether any further funding will be made available to help LEAs implement partnership teaching strategies within the school.

Whole school policies

The move to the mainstream has coincided with a growing realisation that the most important locus for the management of change is the institution rather than the individual teacher. As Riley & Bleach (1985: 78) point out:

> The training of individuals .... and returning them to an unchanged institutional setting all too often prevents them applying what they have learned in their classrooms, let alone in the rest of the school; ... working with one department, no matter how successfully, does not ensure that ideas spread: schools organised on tight departmental lines seldom admit osmosis of ideas.

The (1985) Swann Report reflects this changed perception of the management of change. In outlining various strategies to equip mainstream teachers for their new responsibilities, it draws attention to school-based in-service and enhanced staffing which free teachers to develop skills in language support, either by attending specialist courses or by working alongside LEA advisory staff. The need for the development of team teaching is also stressed. A cascade model is envisaged in which skills are passed on from one colleague to another, making it possible for more and more colleagues to learn ways of supporting language across the curriculum. There is a clear emphasis, then, on whole school change.

Various other developments have increased teacher receptiveness to a whole school approach. Throughout the 1980s, increasing numbers of primary schools introduced whole school planning for topic work which involves the entire staff. The appointment of post holders with responsibility for different curriculum areas has also reinforced the importance of sharing expertise with colleagues. In secondary schools, similar trends can be seen in the creation of cross-curricular posts of responsibility. The introduction of a National Curriculum has underlined the need for whole school policies and planning at both primary and secondary level. Head teachers are required, for instance, to submit long-term development plans which by their very nature encourage a whole school approach. The legal requirement for all children to cover a full range of National Curriculum attainment targets at the various key stages should make it even more likely for team planning to become a reality in order to ensure a co-ordinated approach.

However, the Bourne (1989) survey of LEA provision for bilingual pupils suggests that while whole school approaches are well- established on the level of rhetoric, they have yet to make an impact in practice. The slow rate of development in this area can be explained to some extent by the nature of the Section 11 funding for the education of ethnic minority pupils. It has been permissible, for instance, to use Section 11 monies to provide extra language support staff, but not for other central concerns such as in-service for mainstream teachers or the development of materials. In the absence of central government finance, little professional development has taken place in this area. Despite the far-reaching changes in the organisation and delivery of teaching in the 1980s, only 21% of LEAs responding to the survey reported increases in in-service in relation to bilingual pupils. In the late 1980s, the rapid implementation of the 1988 Education Reform Act (ERA) and the National Curriculum has forced questions of linguistic and cultural diversity to take a back seat.

Even when in-service on mainstreaming is offered, its usefulness inevitably depends on the qualifications and experience of the advisory and language support teachers who have played a central role in staffing and organising courses. The fact that DES (1988) reports that many people working in this field still do not have relevant specialist training is thus a matter of concern. As Bourne (1989) points out, 'It would be facile to suggest that all ESL teachers are equipped to become advisory teachers responsible for in-service development in their school'. In schools where the support teacher is inexperienced, underqualified or not strong enough to take the initiative in negotiating whole school strategies, the level of understanding of recent developments will inevitably be low. This will also be the case when there is a lack of commitment from the head teacher or little interest from the staff.

The difficulties of relying too heavily on language support teachers for the professional development of all teachers further underline the need for such questions to be addressed in a whole-school context. Experience has shown that the recognition of the need for mainstreaming bilingual pupils is most likely to emerge when teachers are involved in reappraisal of school provision from equal opportunities and antiracist perspectives. Bourne (1989) points out that only three out of six primary schools selected for detailed case study had developed their own multicultural, anti-racist or equal opportunities policy, although all the LEAs in which they were found had issued policy statements. Significantly it was only in these three schools that *all* teachers assumed equal responsibility for language development, and developed in-class support strategies in preference to the withdrawal of pupils for extra English language work. Without a whole school policy which looks at the implications of LEA statements on equal opportunities for a given institution, there is no clear framework for the evaluation of existing language policies and practice.

The current situation is far from satisfactory. The philosophy behind the integration of bilingual pupils has been clearly articulated and is sometimes promoted with near missionary zeal. There are many islands of excellence where teachers have adapted their resources and classroom management strategies to meet the challenges of mainstreaming. The overall picture of provision is, however, extremely patchy. The needs of many bilingual pupils, particularly at a secondary level, are often poorly served. Far too many children are being channelled to Special Needs departments, where teachers have little or no experience of second language acquisition, or are left to flounder in classrooms where no attempt is made to develop collaborative learning techniques. The inescapable conclusion is that current arrangements are often no improvement on the segregated provision which was previously on offer. As Bourne (1989) points out:

> If co-operative teaching strategies are to be adopted, it is a matter of priority to develop programmes of curriculum development which involve both teachers and their mainstream partners. The conclusion is not that cooperative teaching strategies are not an effective way of supporting pupils, but that they appeared to be rarely undertaken.

ESL in Canada

The challenge of meeting the needs of children in multilingual classrooms came later in Canada than in UK, but it is interesting to note that the initial reactions followed precisely the same course in both countries. The assimilatory nature of the teaching of English as a Second Language in Britain throughout the 1960s and early 1970s has also been a feature of Canadian schools. Handscombe (1989: 23), for instance, in a discussion of developments within the North York Board of Education points out that:

> The assumption was that the source of difficulty for these students lay in their lack of familiarity with English... It was thought that once the students had learned English they would no longer be at a disadvantage and would be able to be fully integrated into the work of the regular classroom. Hence the creation of special reception or withdrawal programs, the primary aim of which was to teach the new language so that students would be able to benefit from the teaching offered within the mainstream.

Interestingly, special provision in a Canadian context was targeted not only at children acquiring English as a second language but at students of English as a second dialect. This is in marked contrast to the UK where educators were extremely slow in identifying the language needs of African-Caribbean children. The justification for English as a Second Dialect, later renamed English Skills Development, is set out in curriculum guidelines issued by the Ontario Ministry of Education (1988: 23):

> Students who come to Ontario schools from other countries or communities bring with them varied background and a wide range of educational experiences. Some of these students may find themselves at a considerable disadvantage academically because they have not had the opportunity to attend schools regularly. For them opportunities must be provided to upgrade their skills and add to their knowledge in a variety of subject areas. Even those who attended school regularly in their home country may need one or two ESD courses to enable them to enter regular program at a level commensurate with their potential.

The move to a more integrated model has taken place over a much shorter period of time in Canada than was the case in the UK and there is a high level of official support for the benefits of teaching ESL students in the mainstream classroom. At the time of writing, there is no official guidance on ESL for the younger learner from the Ontario Ministry of Education. However, 1988 guidelines for the Intermediate and Senior Divisions state clearly that:

> ESL students .... need many opportunities for interaction with peers and adults, both in and out of the classroom, in order to develop the varieties of English necessary for success in school and in the community. Classroom involvement with other students in large groups, small groups, and pairs encourages language development. All teachers, not just ESL teachers, are responsible for the development of students' language competence (p. 15).

In spite of this endorsement of integration, Ontario currently sanctions three different models of program delivery for ESL and ESD, depending on the academic requirements of the students and the number of students in a school, family of schools or board of education. The first is the intensive support model, targeted at students who have little or no English; or at students who have little or no formal education. Students are expected to spend a 'significant portion of the day' in ESL or ESD classes and the teacher of these classes is responsible for a program which emphasises English, maths and orientation to the new culture. There is also an expectation that students should be introduced to the terminology and basic concepts of geography, history and science as a preparation for integration into the regular program. At the same time, students can be integrated into mainstream classes for those subjects such as physical education, family studies, music and art in which it is assumed that they will be able to participate more readily.

Another possibility within the model of intensive support open to secondary schools with large numbers of new Canadian students is to provide special sections in certain subjects, such as English, history, geography and science. The rationale for the special sections is to help students gain the language skills, specialised vocabulary and conceptual background that they need to study these subjects more successfully in the future. As the debate in the UK has shown, however, intensive support models of this kind limit children's opportunities for interaction with English speakers and risk creating unnecessary segregation. These dangers are certainly recognised by many Canadian educators. A supervisory officer in the Ferndale Board commented on these problems thus:

You're going to the same school but you're still creating a little horde of young people who travel together from their ESL home room to ESL science and ESL math. I can't accept that. I'm hoping that science teachers and maths teachers and tech teachers will start to see how they can spread language across the curriculum, that they can accept responsibility and that they don't have to water down their courses.

The second model is the partial support model, aimed at students who have an intermediate level of facility in English or who have basic reading and writing skills. Students spend up to half a day in separate ESL classes and the expectation is that they are withdrawn from the regular classes during the core instructional time. This partial support – or transition – model would seem to be beset with difficulties. Children in programmes of this kind appear on a register in the ESL classroom. When they are ready to start the integration process, the classroom teacher may already have the maximum number agreed for that grade level and may understandably be upset at the prospect of accepting several new additions. It would also seem that there is considerable reluctance on the part of class and subject teachers to take on responsibility for second language learners who are still perceived to be the charges of the ESL teacher. The fact that children are withdrawn in core instructional time also underlines the fact that they are only being allowed access to a limited curriculum.

The final model is the tutorial support model aimed at students at an advanced level in oral English who still require support in reading and writing; or at those students who have been in an ESD programme and require monitoring as they become integrated into regular classes. These students correspond to British second and third stage learners. The ESL teacher works with the class teacher to design an appropriate program, either teaching students in the regular classroom or withdrawing them for tutorial assistance.

A related question in Canada, as in Britain, concerns appropriate pedagogies. Cummins (1988) argues that a transmission model of teaching confines children to a passive role and induces a form of 'learned helplessness'. He suggests that the more active collaborative learning styles which have underpinned the integration of second language learners in the UK are more likely to empower students. On the level of policy, the Ministry of Education and most boards of education in Ontario support an interactionist approach to learning. However, there is often a disjunction between policy and practice: in many classrooms, the teaching style is still transmission orientated. The model of delivery of ESL is clearly important, since certain arrangements offer more possibilities for interaction than others. However, even with a fully integrated classroom, teaching style remains a central concern. If second language learners form part of mainstream provision but are exposed to teachers who believe their task is to impart a given body of knowledge or a set of skills, the change from segregated to integrated provision is unlikely to make a significant difference to educational outcomes.

Moving into the mainstream in the Ferndale Board of Education

There is thus a great deal of variation in responses to children learning English as a second language in school boards across Ontario. As we explained in Chapter 1, our interest in Ferndale derives from the fact that, at the time of our field study, this board of education had reached a critical crossroads. Ferndale was one of a very small number of boards in Ontario which had formally adopted a policy of mainstreaming for ESL students and was just about to begin the implementation of this policy. Our interviews with teachers, vice-principals, principals, consultants, supervisory officers and the Director of Education are best interpreted as a series of photostills which capture some features of the complex process on which they were embarking. Considerable progress has been made in Ferndale since the time of our fieldwork and the description which follows necessarily represents a narrow slice of time. Its importance lies in the fact that the issues which it raises will continue to be relevant to many Canadian school boards and British LEAs for some time to come.

The first ESL teacher was appointed by the Ferndale Board in 1966. This teacher withdrew groups of students for ESL classes, spending mornings in the school with the highest number of immigrant children, and working as an itinerant teacher in other schools in the area in the afternoon. Numbers of new arrivals increased only slowly and it was not until 1969–70, when ESL student enrolment reached 340, that a group of elementary school principals met to review existing arrangements. They recommended that accommodation for ESL classes should be firmly established; that all immigrant students should be enrolled in the school where the ESL class was located; that ESL students should be bussed to and from their homes; and that students should transfer to their neighbourhood school as soon as possible. It was envisaged that children would integrate into regular classes for approximately half the day in subjects like music and PE in which they could more easily participate. In practice, however, the greatly increased pupil–teacher ratio which resulted from the admission of extra pupils made this system unworkable, particularly in the primary and junior divisions. Although kindergarten children were in fully integrated regular classes, provision for ESL pupils from Grade 1 became increasingly segregated.

At the time of our fieldwork in the Ferndale Board, ESL and ESD had been delivered in almost completely segregated programmes for 20 years. However, the rapid increase in the numbers of immigrants in the 1980s and the concentration of ESL learners in certain areas of the city made it necessary to undertake a second review of programme delivery. A committee of senior staff, centrally employed teachers and elementary principals was set up in 1988/9 to look closely at the current situation. Their recommendations were influenced by a variety of factors, including research findings which pointed to the discriminatory effects of particular types of programme. They were also aware of parental concerns about segregated classes and the disruptive effect of being removed from the home school. Plans for new modes of delivery, which were approved by the Board in June 1989, attempted to address these concerns.

While an integrated model of language instruction was accepted as the ultimate goal, anxieties were expressed as to how this could be achieved, given the level of knowledge and experience of existing staff. In the interim, it was envisaged that a number of different methods of delivery would be used in Ferndale schools. The intensive support model, for instance, would be used at middle school level and in junior schools where space was at a premium. But whereas students had previously spent one to one and a half years in self-contained ESL classes, they would now spend no more than six months to a year after which they would be integrated into the mainstream and receive resource support if necessary.

Simultaneously, attempts were made to increase the number of schools operating a partial support model. This model was envisaged for primary/junior learners and for middle school learners with an intermediate level of facility or basic reading and writing skills. Learners would be taught in separate ESL classes for up to half a day and integrated into regular classes for the rest of the time. This therefore marked a return to the original method of delivery approved by the Ferndale Board in 1969/70 before the pressures of numbers and limited resources resulted in a more segregated ESL programme.

During the transition period, the integrated model which the Ferndale Board wished to work towards was considered appropriate only in schools where principals and teachers indicated a desire to be involved and made the necessary commitment to in-service. In this arrangement, it was envisaged that support personnel would work beside class and subject teachers in the regular classroom. The expectation was that this model would work well in schools with relatively few children requiring ESL support.

In order to enable more teachers to develop the necessary skills to integrate ESL learners, an expansion of appropriate in-service and professional development was planned. Credit-bearing ESL courses custom-designed for regular class teachers from Ferndale who had 'demonstrated a high level of competence in the positions for which they are currently qualified' were to be offered in the evenings, with tuition underwritten by the Board of Education. The role of the ESL consultant was also to be redefined: this officer would be expected to:

> provide support for classroom teachers, to build bridges between ESL and other central support personnel, to recommend and provide resources, to facilitate parental and community involvement and keep school and central staff informed about community expectations, and to co-ordinate school-based in-service so that the importance of language as the basis for all learning is emphasised. (Report of the Standing Committee on English as a Second Language (Elementary) – Alternative forms of delivery, June 14, 1989: 5)

A second ESL consultant was appointed at this time to help in the implementation of these changes.

From policy to practice

The Director of Education made it clear that there was a commitment at the highest level to achieving this transition as rapidly as possible:

> I think it's very important that the senior staff and myself as director speak very positively about this direction and not be ambivalent on it. We need to be supportive of the fact that this is the way we're going and that we're prepared to provide the consultative help to teachers and allocate the professional staff to schools to ensure that this process is successful.

Two main areas of concern surrounding integration emerged clearly from discussions with central support personnel. The first related to the need for staff development in a system which had little or no experience of an integrated model. The second related to staff allocation. A great deal of resistance was expected from some schools on this issue. The proposed changes would mean that large numbers of children currently on the register at schools running ESL programmes would be returned to their neighbourhood schools, a move with considerable financial and organisational implications.

Three main routes for implementing change had been identified. The first involved working through school principals. There was a clear understanding of the central role played by principals both in persuading teachers of the need for change and in ensuring an atmosphere supportive of staff development, summed up neatly in the words of a consultant:

Principals make the difference. The schools that are working effectively usually have a principal and administration that are well- informed about the issues. I prefer going into a school on invitation and
sitting with the principal and the vice-principal or the chairperson and
talking about what's happening, as opposed to talking to a large group
of people and not being quite sure whether all are committed to the
idea... If I were going to facilitate real ownership of an idea, I would
want to have small groups of principals and set it up so that they are
actually talking about what's good for their school. You do that in
terms of 'Here's an idea. What would you do with it?' instead of 'This
is what you'll do'.

The involvement of the principal is clearly crucial in effecting whole
school change. While the commitment of senior staff does not automatically signal widespread consensus or willingness for change, a fundamental reappraisal of policy and practice is more likely to be both rapid and
effective when the necessary structures and organisation are sanctioned by
senior management.

A second route for implementing change was through the consultants
working in all areas of the curriculum at the Board. There was a perception
that responsibility for second language learners needed to be devolved not
only to classroom and subject teachers, but also to consultants, summed
up in the words of one supervisory officer as:

We have to send the message that all people can work with children
of all types in a classroom. There are two people in ESL, but we have
15–20 consultants with program responsibility who can be carrying the
message.

Last but by no means least, in-service was seen as an essential element
in the move to integration. Staff development had been identified as a
priority for the Board and was also recognised as such by teachers. Some
130 principals, vice-principals, senior teachers, ESL teachers and librarians
who took part in workshops on linguistic diversity organised by one of the
present writers in the spring preceding the fieldwork for this project were
invited to comment on their in-service requirements. There was a widespread awareness of the need for information on ESL and for school-based
in-service time which would allow staff to define local problems and
discuss problem-solving strategies. There was also widespread anxiety
that integration was being offered as part of a cost-cutting exercise and that
the levels of resourcing necessary to ensure a smooth transition would not
be made available.

In approving alternative forms of delivery for ESL, the Board had agreed
to fund courses for mainstream teachers in English as a Second Language,

especially geared to the needs of the Ferndale Board. The interest in these courses has been considerable, but even so the proportion of teachers following this path will be low relative to the numbers of teachers working with second language learners on a daily basis. The main priority for ESL programme advisers must therefore be the provision of in-service throughout the Board, for ESL teachers and class and subject teachers throughout the age range. In the short-term at least, it is likely that the limited budget and personnel for the delivery of the in-service program will have done little to relieve the widespread concerns expressed by teachers about their lack of preparation for change.

Working from the bottom up

The strategies employed by senior management entailed building on existing strengths, starting in the elementary school and gradually working up through the age range. Children aged between five and seven were already integrated in Ferndale schools. Active learning situations where children learn through play and experiment were common in primary education and offered an ideal language learning environment. Small class sizes also helped this process: since September 1990, the teacher–pupil ratio for primary classes mandated by the Ontario Ministry of Education has been 20: 1.

By the end of the primary years (five–seven), it is assumed that children will have become fluent in English. It was therefore argued that children with little or no English entering the junior classes would form a much smaller proportion of the total class than they did in the primary years. In addition, primary teachers already experienced in working in integrated classrooms were available to advise colleagues in the junior school embarking on this process for the first time. Some teachers at the junior level, however, expressed concern about mainstreaming. There seemed to be a relationship between teaching style and openness to integration: when teachers used more traditional 'paper and pencil tasks', resistance was often found to be higher.

Certain central support staff and class teachers, however, had a clear vision of the kind of provision they should be offering students. Supervisory officers with special responsibility for this area defined integration as:

> providing access and equity to second language learners in the mainstream classroom with language support. This is evolving all the time. We know where we want to go and that is ESL learners back to the classroom with all teachers being responsible for all learners.

A number of different factors were identified as helping them in their efforts to achieve this end. They felt, for instance, that there was a great deal of bottom-up impetus for the change from both principals and ESL teachers. They pointed to several simultaneous innovations in the mainstream which were supportive of mainstreaming, including learner-centred teaching, peer coaching and an improved model for teacher evaluation. They were also encouraged by the positive demand for in-service provision on mainstreaming. The fact that the University course sponsored by the Ferndale Board had attracted principals, vice-principals, superintendents, and speech and language consultants, as well as classroom teachers was also a cause for optimism, since increasing numbers of people in positions of power and influence now have a greater awareness of ESL issues.

There was certainly evidence of enthusiasm for mainstreaming at a grassroots level. In one school we visited, the ESL teacher and a class teacher, with the wholehearted approval of the principal, had combined their classes and team taught in an open plan area. A project had also been operating in another elementary school since before the board had made the decision to mainstream ESL learners. Here the ESL teacher worked with three class teachers, supporting children both in the home room and in withdrawal groups. Teachers in both these schools were excited about this move to integration. They pointed to the benefits for children who were no longer made to feel isolated, and to the enormous opportunities for teachers to pool resources, share ideas and learn from each other's strengths.

The enthusiasm of committed teachers, however, in no way minimises the enormity of the task before the Board. At the time of our study, the level of awareness among most teachers as to how the changes would be implemented was low. Many people still believed that integration simply meant including ESL students in classes like art and music. Relatively few teachers seemed to understand the implications of integration for all areas of the curriculum, and most felt ill- prepared to cope with this eventuality.

Nor were anxieties confined to mainstream teachers. ESL teachers were often unconvinced either of the need to mainstream or of the workability of this practice. Sometimes this related to feelings of protectiveness towards newly-arrived children and a perception that ESL classes offered a comfortable and necessary cocoon from the 'real world' of the mainstream school or classroom. This concern manifested itself on frequent occasions in references to '*my* children'. Sometimes, resistance to integration resulted from a lack of understanding of the language learning opportunities offered by the regular classroom. One ESL teacher defended her position on half time withdrawal thus:

> I feel I would prefer what I'm doing now. I find that if I want to talk to the class teachers they're right here, though there are children who are

bussed from other schools and I find that a little difficult. I have very good results. This way I can work more closely with them, more on an individualised basis.

There was nonetheless a feeling of optimism about the integration of second language learners in the junior grades. A great deal more concern was expressed about how this would be achieved with older children, for reasons to do with the organisation of secondary education and also for reasons relating specifically to the children in this age range. A supervisory officer crystallised these worries in the following terms:

> My main concern is the intermediate classes. I see those learners – 10, 11, 12, 13, 14 – as being most at risk. I never understood why we try to teach even English first language learners anything at all during puberty! When they often come from tragic backgrounds and they have to learn another language in addition and they're struggling with those hormonal imbalances ... I just see them as drastically at risk. I want to move very, very slowly and carefully and prepare the teachers most particularly at that level.

Teachers at the secondary level expressed a great deal of uncertainty as to how the integration process would work. The greater compartmentalisation of the curriculum in secondary school and less reliance on active learning methods no doubt exacerbated the anxieties which had been expressed even at the elementary level. Even those ESL teachers who were convinced of the benefits of a move to the mainstream sometimes expressed resistance to the idea of total integration:

> There still has to be a place for a reception class. We got three Somalian kids this morning who haven't been in school for three and a half years anywhere. They've never had any exposure to English. There have to be reception classes.

A certain amount of anxiety was also expressed about the reaction of class and subject teachers to integration. As one secondary ESL teacher explained:

> I don't know if the regular day school teachers are ready to have ESL kids in their class. It's going to be a real campaign to sell it. We ESL teachers don't need any more education about ESL. The people who are really going to need the in-service are the people who have never dealt with ESL. There are many around who have never had to adjust their programs. Some of these kids are just going to be lost in the shuffle.

Likely outcomes

A mixed picture emerged from interviews and classroom observation of a wide range of teachers at both elementary and secondary level. On the one hand, there was a palpable feeling of excitement on the part of administrators and of certain teachers that newly-arrived children would be able to take a full part in the mainstream school and to take advantage of the learning opportunities on offer there. On the other hand, there were feelings of hostility, resistance and acute concern at the very wide-reaching changes which were, in most cases, perceived as being imposed from 'on high'.

Such reactions are not wholly surprising. Teachers in Ferndale, as elsewhere, had been told implicitly for a long period of time that only specialist teachers were equipped to teach second language learners. Now, this message was being reversed, and mainstream teachers were being asked to take responsibility for all learners in their classes. In the absence of detailed information on the reasons for change and the implications for classroom practice, a paradigm shift of this nature can be expected to give rise to resistance, disequilibrium, doubts and fears. The task before the Ferndale Board is therefore to provide appropriate information and important first steps have been taken in this direction. There is also a need to address the more general questions of attitude change which have been identified as crucial by writers like Cummins (1988). Recent moves on the part of ESL specialists to work with the race relations department as a way of implementing the Race and Ethnic Relations policy in Ferndale are just one example of developments towards this end.

The chasm between the ideals which have inspired policy decisions to mainstream ESL and actual classroom practice is an ongoing problem for Ferndale, as well as many other Canadian school boards and British LEAs. In the period following a policy decision, there is likely to be a very wide range of quality in delivery, from those totally committed to the ideals of integration and who take appropriate steps to adapt their teaching strategies, to those who perceive the presence of second language learners in their classroom as an unrealistic burden and who take a long time to be persuaded of the need to re-evaluate their classroom practice. In a situation of this kind, it is perhaps legitimate to ask whether second language learners would not fare better in segregated classes. Perhaps a more appropriate question is whether the resource implications of a transition of this kind have been accurately estimated.

Taking stock

The changes in direction observed in the teaching of English as a second language since the 1960s have been extremely far-reaching. We started from an assimilationist stance in which minority languages were seen as a problem: children needed to be given large doses of English by specialist teachers before they would be ready to cope with the demands of the classroom. Theories of language learning have changed dramatically in the intervening years and there has been a growing recognition of the need for bilingual children to be exposed to a wide range of English-speaking models in situations where language is acquired as part of the natural learning process and not necessarily as an end in itself. Concurrent changes have taken place in approaches to education for diversity. The emphasis has shifted from attempts to assimilate ethnic minority children to a recognition of other languages and cultures as an educational resource and an awareness of the need to prepare *all* children for life in a multilingual, multi-ethnic society. This is a theme which will be pursued further in Chapter 5.

There are many differences in local conditions between Canada and the UK. The material and human resources which are available to Canadian schools, including low teacher–pupil ratios, seem too good to be true to British educators who have been on the receiving end of a prolonged period of savage cuts. The high status and sound financial standing of Canadian teachers is in marked contrast with the low ebb in confidence of British teachers, further demoralised by recent educational reform. The conditions enjoyed by Canadian schools contemplating major changes of the kind we have been discussing are thus a great deal more favourable than those experienced by their British counterparts.

Furthermore, since British educators embarked upon the integration process several years earlier, there are many opportunities for Canadian teachers to learn from their mistakes. As a supervisory officer in the Ferndale Board pointed out:

> I was talking reception centre when I first came into this job. I'm now talking about reception process. We *are* learning from other people's experiences. We'll make mistakes. But we'll reduce the number of mistakes by looking at what has happened elsewhere.

The mainstreaming of children for whom English is a second language is not a simple language teaching issue: it has implications for the allocation of staff, for the placement of pupils, for staff training and for building programmes. To what extent, however, will Canadian schools be more successful in achieving effective integration? The answer to both this and to the question of the ultimate fate of mainstreaming in the UK will depend not only on the level of resourcing but on responses to the wider questions which we raise in the next chapter. To what extent are English learning needs seen in isolation? How seriously will schools and teachers respond to the legitimate educational needs of children from culturally and linguistically diverse backgrounds? And to what extent will these needs con tinue to be defined by mainstream White educators rather than by minority communities themselves?

4 Diversity in the Classroom

The present chapter will focus on the ways in which cultural and linguistic diversity demand a reappraisal of the traditional ethos of schools, and of the content and delivery of the curriculum. There have been a number of important developments in this area in both Britain and Canada. Teachers in both countries have begun to question the exclusive focus on English and to consider ways in which children's own linguistic and cultural experiences can be shared and developed rather than suppressed. There is also a growing willingness to work in partnership with parents and community, and an awareness of the dangers of imposing mainstream values and priorities.

Actual classroom practice will depend, of course, on the philosophical stance both of the school as an institution and of individual teachers. Assimilationist views will inevitably be associated with the position that other languages and cultures have no place in mainstream education. A multicultural approach will seek to acknowledge diversity in practical classroom activities and teaching materials. Such an approach, however, will be simply tokenistic, unless curriculum development takes place within a wider framework, one which looks closely at all aspects of school life from an anti-racist perspective.

While there is a long history of bilingualism in Canada and Britain, the presence of multilingual school populations is a more recent phenomenon. Differences in immigration policies, discussed in Chapter 2, have resulted in a slightly longer history of multilingualism in British education. This is reflected, for instance, in a greater volume of British teacher publications and curriculum development in this area. In order to redress this imbalance, references to the Canadian situation will be supplemented by classroom observation and teacher comments collected during fieldwork in the Ferndale Board.

From Assimilation to Anti-racism

As we have already seen, early responses to diverse school populations focussed on the teaching of English, and the children of immigrants were expected to conform to mainstream norms. Until the 1970s, the prevailing view was that diversity was a problem. Only gradually have teachers come to realise that differences in language and culture are potentially an educational resource. The emphasis from this point onwards has been on making the traditional curriculum more responsive to this new diversity.

Classroom practice in the UK

Many accounts of work in British schools in the 1970s are marked by a lively enthusiasm for and excitement about linguistic and cultural diversity. Since the early 1980s, however, criticism of this approach has grown. Many early initiatives, such as the introduction of Black studies courses for African Caribbean children, had been developed to compensate for assumed problems of low self-esteem in Black children (Pollack, 1972; Milner, 1983). Increasingly, however, Black writers such as Stone (1981) and Carby (1980) began to argue that Black children suffer as a result of White racism, and not because of negative self-image. Another difficulty with multicultural approaches was the tendency to simply add new material and practices to an existing curriculum structure, without seriously questioning the structure as a whole. As Massey (1991: 22) points out:

> The disadvantage as many teachers and others saw it, was that multiculturalism became compartmentalised, having little impact on the ethnocentric nature of the rest of the curriculum, and that it frequently sidestepped the issue of racism.

One of the most important conceptual leaps for teachers committed to racial equality in education concerns the move from a tokenistic approach, with the occasional assembly on Diwali, or the inclusion of a Caribbean dish in the cookery class, to the permeation of the curriculum, so that all aspects of school life reflect the diversity of the school and the wider community. The topics chosen for study and the ways in which the teacher approaches these topics are clearly of central concern. Many people now insist that all school topics can be addressed from a multicultural perspective. Ways in which the history and the daily life and experiences of many different cultural groups can be brought to bear on the study of subjects as diverse as mathematics, science, art and music continue to attract the attention of teachers and writers and there is a growing body of practical and theoretical accounts on which practitioners can draw (see, for example, Houlton, 1985; Antonouris & Wilson, 1988; Hessari & Hill, 1989; Edwards, Goodwin & Wellings, 1991).

Classroom practice in Canada

The same uncritical, celebratory approach which we have documented for the UK would seem to hold true for most Canadian schools (Cummins

& Danesi, 1990; Mallea, 1989). As Cummins (1988: 127) points out in
relation to Ontario:

> To many observers it appears that by the time 'multicultural education'
> policies filter down to the classroom, they amount to little more than
> recognition of holidays/festivals from a few cultures in addition to
> those observed by Anglo-Celtic Canadians, and the presence of some
> 'visible minority' referents in textbooks and other curriculum ma-
> terials.

The pattern of responses which is sometimes cynically labelled the
'saree, steel band and samosa syndrome' in the UK certainly seemed
common in schools we visited in the Ferndale Board. A Junior Kindergarten teacher, for instance, expressed excitement about 'the Panjabi suit'
which parents had offered as a present:

> It was very exciting for the parents as a lot of them had never seen a
> non-East Indian woman in a Panjabi suit. It felt beautiful and it made
> me understand why East Indian ladies like to wear them.

A secondary teacher expressed similar enthusiasm for efforts to introduce ethnic food and dance:

> What some of the schools have done is have students bring in their
> foods and have times set aside in class where a student can talk about
> his culture. And almost every culture has a particular dance. You can
> teach the Canadians this is the way we dance. If you can devote a week
> to something like that, I'm sure it's going to help the school in general
> as far as multiculturalism is concerned.

Very many teachers expressed sentiments such as these, most of which
were triggered by the Multicultural Week celebrated in the school, or by
more localised events such as 'Colour Week' where children came into
schools dressed in different colours on four days of the week and tartan on
the fifth, the tartan representing 'the new Canadian spirit as we mixed all
of the colours together'.

A multicultural approach which fails to address the issues underlying
educational underachievement risks being dismissed as ineffective. It is
therefore not surprising to find that the same criticism of tokenism which
has marked debate in British education is also widespread in Canada.
Many educational administrators, consultants and school–community liaison assistants in the Ferndale Board spoke in terms of teachers still being
at the first stage of awareness with an urgent need for personal and
professional development in this area. There is also a keen sense of the
potentially harmful aspects of a multicultural approach. Cummins &
Danesi (1990), for instance, draw attention to the double-edged nature of

multicultural policies and the ways in which celebration of superficial aspects of cultural diversity, such as ethnic food and festivals, may deflect attention from institutionalised racism. This is a concern voiced by Black teachers, too. Our visit to Ferndale took place in the wake of the Black History Month which had been promoted in Board schools. The response of Black teachers was predictably negative:

> Nothing was done at this school. Because I'm the only Black teacher here, I suppose that I'd be the one who was expected to do something about it if anything was going to happen.

> I was invited into a school last week. It was part of the Black History celebrations. I didn't realise that! I guess they needed a Black person in to read the children's books. As soon as I came into the class the teachers left. I was all prepared to have this conversation about books. I wanted to demonstrate to the children that I love books and to pass the books round in the presence of a teacher and the teacher left!

In Canada, as in the UK, there is a growing awareness of the need for a more critical response to multiculturalism and an attempt to produce materials which promote an alternative view (see, for instance, Multiculturalism and Citizenship Canada, 1988). The challenge for British and Canadian educators is clearly to raise the consciousness of practitioners to the limitations and dangers of 'celebratory multiculturalism'. If we are serious in our intent to ensure equality of educational outcome for all children, we need to move beyond this superficial understanding of multiculturalism: attention needs to focus very firmly on the institutional racism which now figures very prominently in analyses of educational policy and practice on both sides of the Atlantic. In the pages which follow, we document attempts to translate the rhetoric of race and education policies into sound classroom practice. There is an urgent need to look closely at existing provision. Do current resources reflect the linguistic and cultural diversity of the school population? What opportunities are there for using other languages and dialects in the classroom? To what extent do teachers work in partnership with parents and minority communities? These are just some of the issues which are fundamental to any attempt to provide a curriculum responsive to the needs of all children.

Resources

Resources are a very important element in the development of relevant learning experiences for all children, and represent a major growth area for British and North American publishers. The volume of learning materials which reflect the diversity of the population at large has grown enormously in recent years. None the less, such resources still constitute only a very small proportion of the stock of most schools and teachers often need to explore a wide range of alternative publishers and booksellers in the quest for materials sensitive to the existence of multi-ethnic populations.

Ethnic minority distributors and community bookshops in the UK stock a wide range of books by Black authors, number and alphabet charts, colouring books of traditional patterns, folk tales and reading material produced in the children's countries of origin. As is the case for English language resources, the quality of these materials is variable and it is therefore important that bilingual colleagues and parents should be involved in evaluation. As one school librarian at the Ferndale Board acknowledged:

> I talk to parents when they come in and ask them if they have any books, whether they can tell me what I should be looking for, that sort of thing. My own ignorance is my biggest drawback. It's just a matter of following every lead you get.

In addition to materials from the countries of origin, there is a wide range of commercially-produced materials from countries like Australia where there is substantial state funding for community language teaching programmes. In the UK, there are also books and teaching packs in a range of languages, produced locally and distributed by teachers' centres, language centres and multicultural support services.

As well as the single language books currently available, there are many dual language texts which allow the same story to be read both in community/heritage languages and in English. Often these are based on traditional folk tales, but there is a growing number of translations of successful non-fiction and picture books first published in English. Such books are often sold together with an accompanying audio-tape. They represent a simple way of adding a multilingual dimension to the classroom and raise the status of languages other than English in the eyes of both monolingual and bilingual children.

Interestingly, monolingual teachers usually respond enthusiastically to publications of this kind. More cynical observers attribute the success of dual texts to the fact that, like many other classroom resources, they do not seriously challenge the principles underlying current practice. The community response has tended to be more guarded. While welcoming the presence of bilingual books in the classroom, some criticism has been voiced about aspects of their presentation (Dave, 1990). The quality of translation is sometimes unsatisfactory. In some cases, publishers use type-setting for English and a handwritten text for the community language, suggesting that the community language has lower status. Difficult decisions have to be taken about the position of the text on the page. For languages like Urdu or Arabic which run from right to left, the minority text is often made to fit English expectations rather than the contrary. The usefulness of dual texts for bilingual development has also been questioned, since bilingual children whose dominant language is English are far more likely to read the text in English than in the community language.

The network of publishers, specialist bookshops and distributors would seem to be a good deal better developed in the UK than in Canada where the resource implications of a multilingual population have been placed on most school agendas more recently. Cummins & Danesi (1990) cite schools such as the Lord Dufferin school in the Toronto School Board and schools in the East York School Board as having significant numbers of books in students' first languages. Students are encouraged to read these books in class and bring them home for reading with their parents. However, attempts to promote the first language in this way would appear to be rare in most Canadian schools. Since many of the British-produced materials are well-suited to Canadian teaching situations, there are clearly many opportunities for interested parties to co-operate both in production and in sharing information on the availability of resources. While dual texts have been an accepted part of the British educational scene for a number of years, they are only just beginning to reach the attention of Canadian schools. Many of the teachers with whom we shared bilingual books reacted with great surprise and excitement, and expressed a willingness to introduce materials of this kind into their classrooms.

All too often, responsibility for materials production is placed firmly on the shoulders of either commercial publishers or specialists, and freely available local resources are overlooked. Neighbourhood shops frequently sell a variety of multilingual material, including cards for the Chinese New Year, Diwali and Eid, comics and newspapers, calendars, posters and advertising materials, printed carrier bags and food packaging, all of which can bring a multilingual flavour to classroom displays. Sarees, salwar kamiz, Afro combs, chappatti pans, chopsticks and other artefacts are all locally available and make invaluable additions which encourage role play in home corners and classroom shops. The tendency to forget these local resources was neatly captured in an anecdote recounted by a consultant with the Ferndale Board:

> One of my teachers was asking where she could find pictures of kids from different cultures? I told her, 'Take pictures of kids in your own school! Look at what's in front of you – they're your best resource!'

The visual environment of a school sends out to children and their parents important messages about the attitudes of teachers and their level of commitment to all children in their care (Edwards & Redfern, 1988; Houlton, 1985). Where are the welcome signs and what languages are they in? Are notices in English only, or are they written in a variety of languages? What kinds of children's work are displayed and are they labelled in more than one language? What are the visual images contained in photographs or posters? Do they reflect a White monocultural society or the multi-ethnic reality of today's world? It is not simply a matter of paying attention to detail of this kind when the teacher happens to remember. If schools are to avoid tokenism, there must be strong multilingual and multicultural elements in all displays and signs, as a constant reminder of the nature of the communities they serve.

The need to use and develop materials which reflect the cultural diversity of present-day society is of critical importance. Given that resources which sensitively mirror diversity are still relatively rare, teachers and librarians in Britain and North America have also found it necessary to critically evaluate their stock from both anti-racist and anti-sexist perspectives. While this more critical approach was a feature of much educational debate throughout the 1970s, the emphasis has gradually changed. Various checklists for the evaluating resources are now widely available (e.g. Preiswerk, 1980; Dixon, 1977; Klein, 1985); some teachers have also begun to involve children in the evaluation process (Goodwin & Wellings, 1991). However, as anti-racist education has become a pressing item on the agenda of both schools and individual teachers, there has also been a growing awareness of the need for resources which facilitate explicit discussion of race and racism. For instance, simulation exercises, suggestions for role play and drama, and photopacks which act as a stimulus for debate are now in use in many schools (Pye, 1991; Redfern & Edwards, 1991; Goodwin & Wellings, 1991).

Using Other Languages and Dialects in the School

In countries where one linguistic and cultural group is numerically and politically dominant, attitudes towards linguistic diversity have traditionally been extremely intolerant. All over Europe, from Catalonia to Wales, from Brittany to Ireland, children using the language of the home at school have, at various times in the past, run the risk of corporal punishment. The same intolerance has also been shown towards non-standard dialects. Cockney and Lancashire and other British English dialects have all been treated with scorn and dismissed as 'slovenly' or 'incomprehensible' or as 'disfigured with vulgarisms' (Edwards, 1983). While children are no longer subject to corporal punishment for using their home languages, negative attitudes to anything which departs from standard are still to be found. As recently as 1970, British teachers exploring the educational underperformance of children of African-Caribbean children described their speech as 'very relaxed like the way they walk' (Edwards, 1983). Similarly misinformed sentiments have been expressed about Black and other non-standard speech in North American contexts (Edwards, 1989).

An important relaxation in this linguistic prescriptivism, however, began to be felt in the 1970s. This was due in no small measure to the pioneering work undertaken by sociolinguists who argued that all languages and dialects are regular, rule-governed systems which adequately fulfil the communication needs of their speakers. In North America, this position was endorsed by the celebrated Ann Arbor case which made it legally binding for teachers to familiarise themselves with the rules governing the language use of their Black students (Labov, 1982).

There is growing acceptance among teachers that children's need to use their native language in the mainstream classroom is legitimate. This position has considerable support from research. Cummins (1983) and Campos & Keatinge (1988), for instance, show that the extent to which students' language and culture are incorporated into the school programme is a significant predictor of academic success. Teachers who attempt to add knowledge of a second language or culture to children's repertoire are more likely to empower students than those who attempt to eradicate the language and culture of the home.

The official response

As we saw in Chapter 1, negative attitudes towards other languages have been the norm in British schools for over a hundered years. Reactions to the diversity of post-war classrooms were a continuation of a long history of linguistic prejudice. Townsend (1971) cites the case of the head teacher who responded to a question about community language teaching in his school with, 'We couldn't start that caper'! Mercer (1981) reports that teachers have been overheard admonishing children speaking Gujarati to each other in the playground to 'stop jabbering'.

None the less, important attitudinal changes have taken place in British schools and the prevailing official climate is one of far greater tolerance towards diversity. A series of government reports on education have contributed to these changes. The (1975) Bullock Report, for instance, promotes bilingualism as an asset which should be nurtured by the school, though guidance as to how this might be achieved was conspicuous by its absence. The (1981) Rampton Report offered more constructive advice, suggesting a 'repertoire approach' which builds on, rather than ignores, the language which children bring to school. The (1985) Swann Report endorses this approach. It talks in terms of linguistic diversity as 'a positive asset' and recommends that all schools should have a role in 'imparting a broader understanding of our multilingual society to all pupils'.

Various reports and guidelines published in the wake of the 1988 Educational Reform Act and in response to the demands of the new National Curriculum (DES, 1984a; 1986a; 1988a; 1989) all seem to accept a repertoire approach to language development, providing that the priority remains the acquisition of written standard English. There is a general consensus that all pupils can benefit from the kind of 'knowledge about language' which can be acquired by sharing information about a wide range of language structures and language use.

The willingness of monolingual teachers and policy makers to recognise and support curriculum development in this area no doubt owes a great deal to the fact that this approach in no way challenges the priority of English as the medium of education. Nor does it detract from the expertise of monolingual teachers. Recognition of genuinely bilingual programmes has been limited to two small-scale and short-term experiments, the first in Bedford (Tosi, 1988), the second in Bradford (Fitzpatrick, 1987).

It would be misleading, however, to suggest that most British schools endorse the use of other languages. Even those schools which have developed race and education policies can sometimes show marked assimilatory tendencies in their response to linguistic diversity. It is by no means uncommon, for instance, for a school to show a high level of awareness of the needs of bilingual children by providing English language support in the mainstream and whole school responsibility for English language development, while giving languages other than English in the curriculum a very low profile (Bourne, 1989). None the less, it is becoming increasingly common for schools to seek ways of using other languages in many different ways.

In Canada, the long history of linguistic intolerance outlined in Chapter 1 has been seriously challenged by recent population changes and government policy has responded to these challenges. French immersion programmes currently serve more than 100,000 children from English-speaking homes. Ukrainian and German bilingual programmes also operate in Alberta, Saskatchewan and Manitoba (Mallea, 1989). British Columbia encourages the establishment of programmes for teaching economically important Pacific-rim languages into mainstream schooling. Some Hebrew–English programmes are to be found in independent schools and there is also one Russian–English bilingual programme within the regular school system (Cummins & Danesi, 1990). There is also official support for bilingual development outside specialist programmes of this

Ontario Ministry of Education (1988: 27) curriculum guidelines, for instance, point out that it is important to recognise:

> the legitimate desire and need for students to use their native language in certain circumstances. English is being added to the language repertoire of students, not replacing it.

In practice, however, there is often a great deal of ambivalence – and, on some occasions, hostility – towards the use of other languages in schools (Samuda, 1979; Cummins, 1988). Comments offered by teachers in the Ferndale Board are illuminating in this respect. At the one extreme, teachers were extremely hostile, though many admitted to having developed a greater tolerance in recent years. In the words of one elementary teacher who talked to us:

> I used to be, 'No! No! Don't do that!' When ESL children would be bumbling away in their own language throughout the recess, I used to say, 'No! No! Speak English!' Then I thought about when I went to Ecuador and everyone was speaking Spanish. It was so nice to be able to speak to somebody in my own language. Now if they talk in class at great length I might say, 'Well let's save that for recess'.

At the other end of the continuum, certain teachers felt quite comfortable with the presence of heritage languages. As one ESL teacher explained:

> I remember a teacher walking by who said to me, 'You know, I heard those boys talking Panjabi!' And I said, 'So? If you and I were suddenly in school as 12 year old boys in India and we got into a Panjabi as a second language class and we knew we could speak English, do you think we'd speak Panjabi?' He said, 'We'd have to'. I said, 'Of course, they're going to speak Panjabi'.

Cummins (1988: 144–5) points out that the diversity of human resources in many communities in Ontario provides the perfect learning environment for a 'genuine multicultural education' which allows for the validation of minority students' experiences in the classroom. He points out, however, that certain conditions need to be fulfilled if this potential is to be translated into reality. Educators must have:

- an additive orientation to students' language and culture such that these can be shared rather than suppressed in the classroom;
- an openness to collaborate with community resource persons who can provide insight to students about different cultural, religious and linguistic traditions; and
- a willingness to permit active use of written and oral language by students so that students can develop their literacy and other language skills in the process of sharing their experiences with peers and adults.

The examples which follow adhere closely to the criteria suggested by Cummins and other writers. They represent attempts to recognise and value linguistic diversity in the classroom and are drawn from the practice of large numbers of teachers in schools both in Britain and in Canada. The greater reliance on British experience, however, is a reflection of the longer tradition of curriculum development for multilingual classrooms in the UK.

Investigating children's languages

In UK classrooms, an important element in the recognition of linguistic diversity has been the development of various 'language awareness' activities which explore children's own language use and attitudes towards the languages of the wider community. A number of influences have given rise to Language Awareness (Jones, 1989). On the one hand, the arrival of New Commonwealth immigrants in the 1960s and 1970s acted as a powerful catalyst for a reappraisal of the language curriculum; on the other hand, a child-centred philosophy of education predisposed many teachers to an approach which builds on rather than rejects or ignores existing knowledge. Advocates of Language Awareness argue that it can help raise the profile of children who speak other languages and dialects by giving them the status of 'experts' in the classroom; it also has the potential for promoting better inter-cultural understanding (see, e.g. Hawkins, 1984; Donmall, 1985; Jones, 1989). Although Language Awareness began in multilingual classrooms, it is now very much a feature of a wide range of schools, where it forms part of the work in modern languages and English. It is also promoted as an activity in its own right.

Developments in this area were endorsed by both the Swann Report (1985), and the Kingman Committee which looked favourably on activities that promote 'knowledge about language' (DES, 1988a). It is easy to understand why activities of this kind have not been perceived with alarm by the establishment. The use of other languages and dialects in the classroom in no way threatens the acquisition of the standard, which remains the primary educational target. It is possible, however, that its potential for challenging the *status quo* has been underestimated. Some writers (e.g. Clark *et al.*, 1991) point out that, while many teachers present Language Awareness as a range of facts about languages, such as language families, or language change, there is no reason that it cannot take on a more critical dimension. There is room, for instance, for taking on board issues of linguistic inequality, racism and sexism in language and the social origins and significance of standard English. Irrespective of the shortcomings of current classroom practice, developments within Language Awareness provide further confirmation that the emphasis has changed from exclusive emphasis on the standard language to viewing the standard as part of a much larger linguistic repertoire.

The language survey has become a very popular element in language awareness activities. Large-scale surveys of linguistic diversity such as the Inner London Education Authority's biennial language census and the more detailed Schools Language Survey mounted in selected education authorities by the Linguistic Minority Project (LMP, 1985) have, over a period of years, made a considerable impact on educational practice. The Schools Language Survey has been particularly influential. By inquiring about dialects as well as languages, the Linguistic Minority Project made it possible to involve all the children in the class and their questionnaire has been adapted for use in large numbers of schools and classrooms.

One of the reasons for the popularity of language surveys is no doubt the range of activities which they generate. It is possible, for instance, to incorporate information on the languages and dialects of the school or the classroom into maths activities such as compiling a histogram, a Venn diagram or pie chart. Children can be encouraged to write about or discuss in groups their language use and attitudes towards diversity.

The effects of language surveys are various. By placing linguistic diversity on the agenda, they raise the profile and status of languages and dialects other than standard English in the school as a whole. The information they provide can help teachers review their resources – do the dictionaries, newspapers and books in classrooms and in the library reflect the range of languages spoken in the school? Equally important, language surveys serve as a means of raising teacher awareness of diversity and can act as a catalyst for curriculum and attitudinal change (Nicholas, 1988; 1989).

There is, however, a need for caution in introducing activities of this kind. Given the history of ignorance and neglect of language varieties other than standard English, children may react with great suspicion. This danger is particularly marked in the case of Black children whose ethnically marked speech is subject to very strong stigmatisation. Teachers interested in investigating children's language have found that it is essential to establish their own favourable attitudes to diversity and an atmosphere where differences can be discussed openly and with mutual trust. It is also essential to offer opportunities for all children to take part. If activities are confined to bilingual children, monolingual children may perceive this to be an area which is marginal to their own interests and experience, while bilingual children may resent the feeling of being placed 'on display'.

Houlton (1985:12), for instance, reports the kind of problems which teachers sometimes meet:

> One boy has so far shown disdain ... his father is a senior figure in the local Urdu-speaking community and has said he wants nothing to do with it at all. A girl says she's afraid of being laughed at by me and the other children if she says anything at all in Urdu. Of the two West Indian girls one has parents born in Barbados and insists they never speak anything but standard English. The other has parents of Jamaican origin who speak 'patois' but at the moment she is very reticent about it .... Perhaps they think we are meddling in their private affairs.

However, it is the experience of many teachers that, when handled with sensitivity, children respond enthusiastically to investigations of their language; they are happy to display and share their experience as language users.

Linguistic diversity across the curriculum

Language surveys are, of course, just one means of introducing other languages into the classroom. As the example of the Urdu speaking child suggests, if learning about language diversity is to be a natural and accepted feature of school life, it needs to permeate the curriculum as a whole, as well as being an interesting area of study in its own right. A great deal of thought and imagination have been invested in exploring ways in which languages other than English can form a natural and spontaneous part of life in schools. Various curriculum development projects in the UK throughout the1980s have tried to raise teacher awareness of linguistic diversity and the ways in which bilingual pupils can be encouraged to draw on home languages, not only to support their own learning but also to promote linguistic awareness among monolingual peers. Such projects include the Schools' Council 'Mother Tongue Project' (1981–1985) which focussed on the needs of the multilingual classroom, and the EC-funded 'Linguistic Diversity in the Primary School Project' (1986–9) which explored the teacher training implications of linguistic diversity. An awareness of multilingual issues also permeates the materials produced by the National Writing and National Oracy projects.

There is evidence that national initiatives have started to make an impact on classroom practice. For instance, Edwards, Goodwin & Wellings (1991) point to the use of community languages in multilingual role play and drama to considerable effect. Richardson (1982) discusses the usefulness of grouping children from the same language background for small group work on topics such as inter-generational conflict, where the use of the home language would be most natural. Developments in this area have received limited support from the two official reports on the teaching of English which preceeded the publication of the National Curriculum document on English. Both the Kingman Report (DES, 1988a) and the Cox Report (DES, 1989a) acknowledge the value of bilingualism and suggest that the knowledge and experience of bilingual children can be shared in the classroom to the benefit of all children.

Houlton (1985) also points to a variety of practical approaches to linguistic diversity across the curriculum. The use of other languages can form a natural element in the study of writing and number systems, cookery, accents and dialects, names and naming systems, games and songs, poems and rhymes. Many themes for topic work – Ourselves, Communication, Food, Our Neighbourhood, Festivals – also lend themselves to learning about language, and even topics which do not have an overtly linguistic or cultural bias can offer opportunities for discussing language. Take, for instance, this description from Houlton (1985) of topic work on birds:

> In the lower junior classes language diversity has become an element in topic work, this term on birds. Stories have been the main means of developing language awareness within this theme. A little French book, *Printemps*, provided images of the coming spring with the appearance of the swallow. Clear strong shapes in the illustrations were used in painting and cut-out silhouettes. *Ma Sparrow's Babies* in English and Bengali has a chorus which is repeated throughout the cumulative storyline and characters are named in the Bengali words for their occupations. *The Two Cockerels* in English and Yoruba proved a source of interest. Most children were amazed to learn that Yoruba is just one of many, many African languages, and were intrigued that they could identify the meaning of a few Yoruba words with the help of the parallel English text.

> Tracing migratory patterns of birds brought opportunities to identify language areas, to talk about the geographical 'continuum' of language communities and briefly, to relate bird migration to the migrations of people within and between countries and the resultant 'borrowing' among languages.

Attempts of this kind to incorporate other languages and dialects into the classroom inevitably meet on occasion with hostility on the part not only of teachers but also of some parents. English parents sometimes express concern that their children will suffer; bilingual parents, too, sometimes want their children to be exposed only to English. In situations such as this, a whole school approach is essential. Teachers need to take account of parents' views and wishes in devising their school policy. They also need to spend time discussing and working out the rationale for their approach so that they can communicate to all concerned the reasons why their classroom practice is beneficial for all children, monolingual and bilingual alike.

Learning other languages

Another way of promoting linguistic diversity in the school is for teachers to begin to learn one or more of the languages spoken by their pupils. In the UK, many teachers' centres offer classes in the most commonly spoken minority languages in their area for those who wish to follow a more formal course of study. Language classes for English speakers are also offered by various community organisations and in colleges, and a successful Urdu course has now been developed for radio (Khan & Siddiqui, 1988). The Inner London Education Authority developed a collection of useful greetings, phrases and questions in a variety of languages for use with newly arrived children. There are also many informal opportunities to learn functional language of this kind in conversation with children and their parents.

Attempts to learn minority languages need to be approached with care. In schools where many different languages are spoken, do teachers learn some basic expressions in all the languages spoken or do they choose to study one language in greater depth? If they decide to learn a language more formally, which variety of the language do you speak? Italian children in Britain and in Canada will almost invariably come from homes where a dialect and not the standard language is spoken; Bangladeshi children in Britain will usually speak Sylheti, not Bengali. If teachers decide to learn informally in the classroom, children and parents may feel embarrassed or patronised if they do not feel confident about the school's general approach to linguistic diversity.

In spite of these potential pitfalls, many teachers attach great importance to this aspect of their work and claim benefits for themselves and for the children. By placing themselves in the role of learner, they begin to understand just how difficult it is to speak a second language proficiently; they also appreciate the kinds of pressures to which many children are exposed on a daily basis. As a librarian consulted in the Ferndale Board pointed out:

> I make a point of greeting the child in his own language. It's a nice way to make contact because I ask them how do you say this and they're more than happy to teach me. They like to laugh at my accent and correct me or whatever.

Reports of children being more willing to use the language of the home, and parents' obvious pleasure in the teachers' interest in their language are also commonplace when teachers have made the effort to learn and use the languages of their pupils (Houlton, 1985).

Bilingual support

Bilingual support teaching represents by far the most radical approach to using other languages in British schools. The best source of information on current practice in this area comes from the NFER survey of LEA provision for bilingual pupils. Bourne (1989: 148–9) divides the kind of activities undertaken by bilingual support teachers into three main categories, with most teachers or 'assistants' undertaking all three at different times:

(a) *Individual support for pupils in the class*: where unqualified assistants were employed in schools there was sometimes a concentration on helping individual pupils newly arrived in England, or in other classes, on helping 'slow learners' with their work. It would seem important to think through the 'hidden curriculum' involved in this in terms of pupils' perceptions of the status and value of other languages in the society and in learning.

(b) *Translating work*: bilingual teachers and assistants undertook tasks such as labelling displays in two or more languages; making bilingual notices, preparing audio tapes in other languages, and working with pupils to translate their own work for dual language texts.

(c) *Whole class work*:

(i) leading the class – a number of lessons were observed which included bilingual story telling sessions; in one case a bilingual support teacher led a class developing work on spices, but added to her multicultural education objectives by including work on calligraphy, with all pupils writing the names of the spices in Panjabi;

(ii) in partnership – full tandem teaching of lessons which the bilingual support teacher or assistant had been fully involved in preparing, involving the full class and linguistically mixed groups of pupils; with the bilingual teacher using both English and another language as they moved around the groups. The tasks sometimes involved written work in other languages, or sometimes it was left to pupils to choose how to record their work.

As a newly developing area, support teaching is not surprisingly beset with difficulties, many of which are reminiscent of the kinds of problems described by English language support teachers in Chapter 4. Recent and ongoing research in this area (Thompson, 1991; Martin-Jones & Saxena, 1990) will hopefully point to more positive models of co-operation. On a practical level, some bilingual support teachers complain, for instance, that they have received no adequate job descriptions and therefore are unclear as to the exact nature of their role. Another common complaint is that they are not sufficiently involved in lesson preparation. Even when this is not the case, bilingual support teachers, like English support teachers, have insufficient time for liaison with class teachers.

There are also questions of status. Bourne (1989) reports that some bilingual teachers resist attempts to involve them in bilingual support because they fear marginalisation. Nor does the fact that many bilingual support teachers are actually unqualified assistants help enhance the prestige of bilingualism in school. This is clearly a matter which requires the urgent attention both of local authorities and central government. (See next chapter for related discussion on the status of community language teachers). A whole school approach which encourages discussion and clarification of such issues for all teachers is clearly a prerequisite for progress in this area.

There has been significant movement throughout the 1980s towards the notion of 'multilingual education', the aim of which is to encourage children to make use of the full range of their linguistic repertoire in communication and in learning, with the support of multilingual teachers, assistants, parents and resources. This approach in no way challenges the centrality of English as the main medium of education and the importance of providing English language support for bilingual children across the curriculum.

There is, however, a growing tension between the official view of what constitutes appropriate education for bilingual pupils and the view of many teachers and community organisations. It has become increasingly clear that central government considers the use of home languages simply as a bridge to the acquisition of English, and not as a legitimate educational activity in its own right. The Swann Report (1985), for instance, considers that bilingual support is appropriate in primary education, but pays no attention to its possible applications in the secondary school. This position has been reinforced by new criteria for Section 11 funding which are likely to result in significant cuts in mother tongue and bilingual provision.

Working with Others

Activities designed to promote other languages and cultures in schools need to take place in an atmosphere of acceptance and mutual trust. In order to achieve this end, good communication with parents is essential. In the final section of this chapter, we aim to explore the fundamental importance of partnership with parents and community, and the critical role which this plays in ensuring that the languages and cultures of all children in the school enjoy the respect which they deserve.

Effective communication with parents has long been a major part of school policy in both Canada and the UK, but the strategies employed and the success enjoyed by different schools are highly variable. In a Canadian context, Cummins (1988) characterises teacher attitudes towards community participation along a collaborative-exclusionary dimension. Teachers operating at the collaborative end of the continuum actively encourage parents to become involved in classroom activities and draw upon the help of community/heritage language teachers or aides to ensure effective communication. Teachers operating at the exclusionary end of the continuum, in contrast, are likely to dismiss parental involvement as irrelevant or even harmful and will look on teaching as *their* job.

There is usually a great deal of good will on the part of teachers and considerable frustration that their efforts are not rewarded with better attendance at parents' evenings or greater participation in school events. All too often in these cases, there is a failure to recognise the structural constraints which work to hold parents at a distance. As Handscombe (1989: 26) points out, 'involving parents as partners requires staff to engage parents in dialogue which goes far beyond the exchange of formulaic pleasantries'.

The extent of work which remains to be done in this area is clearly illustrated by the results of research undertaken by the Ferndale Board of Education. In the review of the implementation of the Race and Ethnic Relations policy, half of secondary and almost two thirds of the elementary teachers surveyed reported that few or no parents from ethnic communities attend school-related meetings. In a similar vein, over half of secondary and a quarter of elementary teachers reported that few or no parents from ethnic communities attend school functions such as concerts and sports events.

The ways in which schools interact with parents is a faithful reflection of whether they value their presence. Teachers in Britain and in Canada frequently complain about the failure of minority parents to respond to invitations or to initiate contact with the school. There is no shortage of evidence, however, that, when teachers treat parents as equal partners in their children's education, such barriers can be overcome (Tizard, Scholfield & Hewison, 1982; Edwards & Redfern, 1988).

Sometimes quite simple steps can bring about very striking changes. In many British schools, for instance, the head teacher makes a point of being at the main entrance to greet parents and children both as they arrive and also at the end of the day. One consequence of this policy is that the head gets to know a wide range of families well. Edwards & Redfern (1988: 69) describe this process in a Reading primary school in the following terms:

As the bell rang at five to nine, [the head teacher] would be there without fail at the entrance, greeting the children and parents. And again as the children were collected at half past three, he would be there, gradually getting to know the families better and better as the days went by, remembering the details they told him and asking them the next day about the outcome.

Another consequence of this arrangement is that, instead of needing to make an appointment, or waiting for a crisis, parents feel free to raise matters of concern as and when they arise.

Another simple move which ensures better communication with parents is the open classroom policy adopted by increasing numbers of schools where there is an expectation that parents come into the classroom at the beginning or at the end of each day to share their children's work. The traditional lines of demarcation – teacher to one side of the door, parents to the other – are broken down and the greater contact encourages a sense of partnership between school and home.

Arrangements such as these work well in British primary schools which are traditionally within walking distance of the home. They cannot be as effective, of course, in cases where a high proportion of children come by bus, or with the families of older children who make their own way to school. None the less, this example points to the difference which quite simple structural changes have made in parents' willingness to make contact with the school.

The more widespread use of the telephone in Canada struck us, as British researchers, as a possible additional element in the armoury of teachers keen to establish good relations with parents. Our only reservation about this means of communication is our own preference, as Europeans, for face-to-face contact and our own experience of the extra strains which phone calls create when speaking in another language. We imagine that many ethnic minority parents would share these anxieties. However, we also recognise that the tremendous reliance on the phone in Canadian society is likely to bring about a rapid change in attitudes in many newcomers. Teachers we consulted often spoke of how they would call parents if there was a problem or if they wished to inform them of an event; several said that they gave their own home numbers to parents and encouraged them to make contact if they had any worries. It would seem, however, that teachers are sometimes reluctant to make contact with ethnic minority parents in this way. The ESL programme adviser at the Ferndale Board, for instance, spoke of her frustration on calling a Tanzanian parent to discuss his child's difficulties to find that he had no idea that there was a problem:

He was outraged.... Each time I say to the teacher, 'Are you letting the parents know, are you phoning home?' We have to communicate with parents.

Another area which has rightly attracted a great deal of attention is schools' admissions procedures. Significant advances have been made in this area: many schools organise parents' meetings which explain the policies and practices of the school; often schools arrange for teachers to make home visits before the child starts school. Edwards & Redfern (1988: 91), for instance, describe the operation of home visits in Redlands Primary School thus:

> When I first mention the home visits to people outside the school, they often think that parents might object and see it as a way of spying on them, their home, their provision for their children and so on. Nothing could be further from the truth. The idea was to meet the parents on their home ground, somewhere where they felt completely at ease and where we hoped to be accepted as persons in our own right, not just as teachers. It is the family we are interested in and not the choice of curtain material.

The presence of a multilingual, multi-ethnic population also has important implications for record keeping. Certain details – such as date of birth and children's and parents' names needs to be collected with great care and sensitivity because of varying practices from culture to culture. Schools also need information on diet and eating traditions to ensure that suitable school meals can be provided and also so that curriculum work on food can draw on the children's own experience.

Religion is another area which requires sensitive handling. At the time we undertook field work in Canada, the issue of whether Sikh boys should be allowed to wear the kirpan (dagger) was causing a great deal of alarm among teachers in many parts of Ontario, largely because its ceremonial and religious significance had been misunderstood. At roughly the same time, a British secondary school was making headlines by excluding two fundamentalist Muslim sisters who wished to cover their heads for religious reasons. This reaction marked the resurrection of an issue which most British educators believed had been resolved in the 1970s. Variation in clothing for religious reasons had proved a serious challenge in British schools, many of which have a tradition of imposing discipline through a prescribed school uniform and regulations about hair styles and jewellery. The gradual understanding of the religious importance for Muslim girls of covering the legs, however, led to the unlikely compromise of permitting girls to wear salwars in school colours. Although the salwar was no longer a bone of contention, the newer issue of covering of the head led to the same process of confrontation, pointing both to the conservatism of the dominant group and to the very lengthy process of change which is involved in adjustment to the needs of cultural pluralism.

Meetings at school often prove a stumbling block and, again, significant efforts have been made to identify the various practical and structural factors which prevent parents attending. These inevitably include the timing of meetings and the problems which this often poses for parents working shifts. The venue for the meeting can also be important. A consultant at the Ferndale Board described the great success which she had experienced when meetings were moved outside the school:

> In my other board we had parents' groups. They were set up according to language. Each staff member took on a particular group. I worked with the Spanish group. We met in the apartment building in the social room rather than in the school. And the principal was always present with 2 or 3 staff members who volunteered to go along. We did it collaboratively. It made our school life so much easier. They informed us of what they thought was important. We were eager to tell them about the curriculum and how they could help.

Attempts to consider alternative venues for parent meetings, however, would seem to be the exception rather than the rule. The research undertaken in the Ferndale Board on the implementation of the Race and Ethnic Relations Policy revealed that more than four fifths of secondary and two thirds of elementary teachers surveyed reported that they have never used sites outside the school for meetings with parents.

There has also been a great deal of experimentation with the format and kind of events which are offered to parents. Informal meetings which allow parents 'hands-on' experience tend to be a great deal more popular with parents than the more traditional formal talks. On many occasions, however, teachers have a low level of awareness as to why such events are intimidating for parents; they also tend to show a limited awareness of cultural differences in behaviour on these occasions. Any teacher who has attended a Sikh *gurdwara*, for instance, realises that it is accepted practice for young children to roam freely or for worshippers to talk among themselves. Such an understanding throws light on why the behaviour of many Indian parents in concerts contravenes Anglo-Canadian expectations:

> We've got away from having concerts because parents come with their young children, their babies, their toddlers and they'd chat to their neighbours all through the concert. We had worked on having short assemblies throughout the year to teach the children as an audience that you were to *listen*. This was not a concept that parents at this level

had at all. We've moved away from this. What we have now is gymnastics with equipment set up, we have programs in the classrooms where a class might do a poem or display about something they've done so parents move around. But still the parents chat and are noisy and not really tuned to listen.

There is, however, evidence of a greater understanding on the part of many teachers, both in Canada and in the UK, of the ways in which contact with parents and community can help the school respond more sensitively to the needs of changing populations. The intransigence and resistance to change which is found in many different quarters is tempered to some extent at least by feelings of excitement about new possiblities. The following remarks by a school librarian in the Ferndale Board are typical of this more positive approach:

> We have a very strong video camera club here. They document just about everything in the school. We could dub those films in a number of different languages. I'd like to involve volunteers from the community, because I think that would bring in parents or aunts or uncles and they would see this as their school. Frequently parents are afraid, intimidated – and why not! We're the bureaucracy, they're from another culture. In some cultures you don't interfere, so we need to reach across that boundary.

Some British LEAs employ community education officers with a brief to improve relations between minority communities and the school and to increase parental participation in their children's education. This same role is fulfilled in larger school boards in Canada by school-community liaison officers. Cummins (1988), however, points to the potential conflict of interest which arises for people in this role who identify concerns which may be at odds with the interests of the school board. An interesting case in point is the attempt by the Toronto Board between 1984 and 1986 to integrate heritage language teaching into the regular school day (for further discussion, see Chapter 6). Charlie Novogrodsky, the co-ordinator of the School Community Relations (SCR) Department explained the difficult position in which his staff found themselves in terms of:

> a classic confrontation between on the one hand, a heartfelt community desire (in many hearts) to have their culture and language recognised as part of the regular school curriculum through an integrated program: that desire coming up against an equal desire, on the other hand, on the part of the people who are closest to the work – teachers – to control the condition, including the time and scheduling under which they deliver their work. (*Roll Call* 8.3.1986, quoted in Cummins, 1988: 154)

Significantly, the SCR department was disbanded following the election of new school board trustees in 1985 and Charlie Novogrodsky left his post of co-ordinator 'because of the unavailability of work' (*Roll Call*, November 1986: 8). In order to avoid the tensions sometimes generated by the present system, Cummins suggests a system of 'community advocates', independent of the school boards, who would be free to advise parents in their own languages and also to represent them at times when important decisions are being made about their children's future.

Parent volunteers

Teachers tend to involve parents in the same range of activities in both Canada and Britain. Parents are most often used for listening to children reading, in taking small groups for cooking, in fund-raising activities, in the library and as helpers on school outings. Most parent volunteers tend to be used in servicing roles and low status activities outside of the core curriculum. The level and kind of involvement, however, tend to vary a great degree from one school to another.

When schools have successfully negotiated the structural blocks which stand in the way of good communication, initiatives involving parents flourish and often assume far more imaginative and exciting dimensions. Developments in British schools in recent years include the use of bilingual parents in story-telling activities; a proliferation of home-school reading schemes (Wolfendale, 1983) where children read to parents who communicate with teachers via a message book; parents' mornings in which parents work alongside their children in the classroom (Edwards & Redfern, 1988); and parents' writing groups where parents write stories for their children in English and in other languages. There has also been a marked movement towards ensuring that parents' perceptions of their children's interests and abilities are incorporated into the formal record-keeping process (Barrs *et al.*, 1988).

Interpretation and translation

When dealing with populations which include members who are fluent in languages other than English, there can be no doubt of the need for translators and interpreters at all levels of communication between home and school. The Anglocentric underpinning of many schools, however, sometimes makes it difficult for teachers to understand the vulnerability of parents who are not completely at ease with English and their apparent reluctance to become involved in their children's formal schooling. The following extract from an interview we conducted with an elementary school principal at the Ferndale Board clearly illustrates the problem:

Principal: We had 16 people turn up to view our video on reading. It was a really dreadful rainy night so we were quite pleased with that.
Researcher: Is the sound track for the video available in other languages?
Principal: There's no voice over in anything but English. It needs to be elaborated by someone who understands what's going on.
Researcher: You had a translator at the meeting?
Principal: No, we didn't
Researcher: Were there a lot of parents who were finding it difficult to understand the English?
Principal: No but there may be people who didn't come.

The interview in no way demonstrates either indifference or hostility to the ethnic minority parents in this principal's school. It does, however, underline the low level of perception of what it is like to function in a society where your command of English is limited.

A bilingual teacher consulted during fieldwork at the Ferndale Board pointed to how basic a worry this is for many parents:

Only three parents came for interview. So I got on the phone to every parent. I said, 'That's your child and we have to work together'. They'd say, 'I can't speak English'. I said 'I'll speak with you in Panjabi' So I speak Panjabi to most who come for interview.

This teacher was able to use her own bilingualism to good effect. Monolingual teachers must, of course, rely on interpreters and translators. In doing so, they demonstrate in a simple and straightforward way their intent to treat parents as equal partners in their children's education.

The use of interpreters and translators does require special thought. There is, for instance, a need for lead time when meetings are planned or when messages are sent home. When emergencies arise the temptation will be to draw on the services of a bilingual colleague or a parent, but it is important to avoid imposing on people who are often very busy or who may be too polite to say no. Careful attention also needs to be given to who will act as interpreter when the school needs to discuss a difficult issue. Parents may well wish to choose their own interpreter in a situation of this kind.

The low level of awareness of the importance of translation and interpreting which is often to be found both in Canada and the UK can be attributed to some extent at least to the model offered by educational administrators and policy makers. To our knowledge, no British LEA policy document on race and education has been made available in languages other than English. Until recently, Canadian educators have been similarly remiss. As a superintendent in the Ferndale Board commented:

If the schools are going to believe that it's an important thing to do, we have to be doing it ourselves and we don't. Even our ethnic and race relations policy was only available in one language. I took the opportunity to get the review of the implementation of the policy translated into eight languages centrally and then said to the schools, if you need another language other than the major ones that we've chosen, then by all means go ahead and we will pay the translation costs. So we've started to model for the first time ever that this is something that we believe in and that we value and so hopefully this is something that will spill over into the schools

Re-inventing the Wheel?

This chapter has attempted to identify problems and challenges in relation to cultural and linguistic diversity which face British and Canadian teachers. The most common response to diversity in both countries has been described as 'celebratory multiculturalism' – the tendency to focus on superficial differences, such as festivals and foods, without any critical awareness of the institutional racism which is now widely acknowledged to play a major role in the underachievement of ethnic minority children. If schools in Canada and in the UK are serious in their intent to ensure equality of educational outcome for all children, there needs to be an acknowledgement of the dangers of tokenism and a more critical appraisal of the content and delivery of the curriculum.

Some significant progress has been made in attempts to permeate children's learning experiences with multicultural, multilingual perspectives. The question of relevant and appropriate resource materials, for instance, has been placed firmly on the agenda in many British and Canadian schools. There have also been important initiatives in curriculum development in the area of language, especially in the UK with its longer history of provision for multilingual school populations. No doubt as a result of this longer history, many of the classroom practices which are now commonplace in British schools, including bilingual support and the promotion of community languages across the curriculum, have yet to make an impact in Canadian classrooms. Other developments, including whole school policies and the implementation of anti-racist policies in all-White schools, are also more advanced in the UK than in Canada for the same reason.

Changes in immigration legislation in the UK mean that there are now relatively few new arrivals in British schools. Consequently, many of the challenges which face Canadian teachers are no longer pressing issues in British schools. Differences in the nature of the minority populations in the two countries, however, fade into insignificance when placed beside the core of common experiences. Many developments in the UK in the last thirty years may well have relevance for Canadian teachers today. By the same token, the greater level of spending on education and more favourable work conditions in North America may give rise to Canadian solutions which will be of considerable interest to British teachers. If we are to avoid re-inventing the wheel, there are opportunities both to share achievements and to learn from mistakes. It would be extremely short-sighted if teachers, administrators and policy makers on both sides of the Atlantic failed to pool experiences and resources.

5 The Teaching of Minority Languages

In the previous chapter we looked at ways in which the exclusive emphasis on English is gradually giving way to a more liberal approach in which the languages and dialects which children bring to school are viewed as an educational resource rather than a problem. While such an approach acknowledges the benefits of bilingual and biliterate development, it does relatively little to promote it. The present chapter examines more focused attempts on the part of both school and community to transmit minority languages, generally known as 'heritage languages' in Canada and 'community languages' in the UK.

The differing political conditions in Canada and Britain have given rise to different patterns of language teaching provision. In the UK, where ethnic minority communities still represent a relatively small proportion of the overall population and have little political influence, the main responsibility for teaching minority languages has been placed very firmly on the shoulders of minority communities themselves. In Canada, however, the rapid growth of linguistic minorities in recent years has resulted in more political power for 'new Canadians', and has made it possible to demand greater recognition and support from mainstream education.

We will look at the many problems which beset the teaching of minority languages in both countries and we will suggest that, despite better organisation and resourcing in Canada, heritage language teaching in this North American setting remains, as it is in the UK, a marginal concern.

Reasons for Promoting Bilingualism

In order to understand the polarisation surrounding the teaching of minority languages, it is important to provide an historical context. Traditionally, the attitudes of mainstream educators towards bilingualism have been dismissive. A widely-held tenet of folklinguisitics, despite research evidence to the contrary, is that the brain has only a finite capacity and that, therefore, bilingual children learn neither language as well as they might if they had confined themselves to one language. A large number of studies undertaken in Britain and North America between the 1920s and 1960 promote this view of bilingualism as an intellectual handicap (Darcy, 1953; Peal & Lambert, 1962). However, such studies often have serious methodological flaws. Sometimes they compare middle class monolinguals with working class bilinguals from poor areas with under-resourced schools; sometimes they fail to take into account that one language is nearly always more dominant than another and test children in their weaker language. More recent research (see Hamers & Blanc, 1989 for an overview) suggests a very different picture, pointing to the intellectual and cognitive benefits arising from bilingualism.

It is also significant that bilingualism is considered a disadvantage only for children who belong to immigrant and minority language groups. In other situations, quite different attitudes prevail. Take, for instance, the 'élite' bilingualism of those schools in Wales which teach predominantly through the medium of Welsh and which successfully attract children from English-speaking homes; or of the French immersion programmes in Canada, where the ability to speak two languages is felt to be an asset by English-speaking families. The educational successes of children in programmes of this kind are simply not compatible with the notion that bilingualism is an intellectual handicap.

Negative attitudes towards bilingualism are, however, inextricably entwined with attempts to maintain the *status quo*. Dominant ethnic or linguistic groups are often quick to realise that support for minority languages and cultures is a potential threat to their power base. Of course, opposition to minority languages is not usually justified in terms of power relations. More often the need to assimilate is explained on economic grounds, or in terms of the socially divisive nature of promoting minority concerns, or as being in the best educational interests of newcomers.

Over the years, however, various arguments have been articulated by members of minority communities and educators alike in support of bilingualism. These arguments have three different foci: the individual, the minority community and the wider society.

On an individual level, the promotion of bilingualism has been justified from several points of view (Houlton & Willey, 1983; Cummins & Danesi, 1990). Despite fears that continued use of the home language may have a detrimental effect on second language acquisition, there is evidence that a sound foundation in the first language in no way impedes this process (Fitzpatrick, 1987). On the contrary, research findings indicate cognitive benefits for bilinguals, such as greater success in acquiring subsequent languages (Cummins, 1984). Also on the level of the individual, it is widely argued that a sound foundation in the language(s) of the home increases children's self-esteem and confidence in their own ethnicity; that the use of the home language is an important support for relationships within the family and the wider ethnocultural community; and that the individual's vocational and life options are greatly extended by the ability to speak other languages.

When we move from the individual to the minority community, it is not difficult to see that the larger group can survive as a distinct entity only if the next generation continues to identify with it. The ability to speak the home language allows children to benefit from contact not only with parents and grandparents but gives access to the collective history to which the child's own history can also contribute (Cummins & Danesi, 1990).

Bilingualism also has implications for society as a whole. In a school environment where linguistic diversity is seen as an asset rather than a problem, positive exposure to other languages can have benefits for all children, since such an approach supports children's confidence in their own linguistic repertoire and increases their level of language awareness (DES, 1988a). It can contribute to combating racism by raising awareness of cultural diversity and by improving communication between different cultural groups. It has also been argued that, outside the school environment, everyone will benefit from the self-confidence which results when individuals have a strong sense of their identity, both as members of an ethnolinguistic minority and as members of the wider society. People who speak more than one language are in a strong position to contribute to the country's economic growth and political well-being as it takes its place in an increasingly interdependent world.

Running through the arguments for the benefits of bilingualism is an assumption that certain principles are important. For instance, various British LEAs, including Berkshire and the now defunct Inner London Education Authority, have developed race and education policies which specifically link a positive response to bilingualism with the promotion of equality and justice. Links have also been made between race and education policies and child-centred education (Houlton & Willey, 1983). In both cases, there is an assumption that teachers should build on the skills and knowledge that children bring with them to school. In this view, acceptance of linguistic diversity is an essential feature of all good educational practice.

Against this background of polarised views on bilingualism, and the political considerations which underlie them, we turn now to the attempts of linguistic minority communities in the UK and Canada to pass on their language and culture to the next generation and the responses of the education systems in both countries to these efforts.

Community Language Teaching in the UK

A variety of terms, including 'first languages', 'mother tongues', 'home languages' and 'community languages' have been used over the years to describe languages in addition to English spoken by various ethnic minority groups in the UK. The terminological confusion is a clear reflection of the complexity of this subject. Italian, for instance, cannot be described as the first language or the home language of children who have always spoken English with their parents but who go to classes in the language of their wider ethnocultural community. Moslem children who speak Panjabi in a family context may well attend classes in Urdu, the language of 'high culture'. A language studied in a formal situation of this kind cannot, however, be described as a 'mother tongue'. 'Community languages' avoids many of these pitfalls by moving the focus from the individual family to the wider community. This term is therefore used in the discussion of ethnic minority languages in a UK setting, in preference to the various other terms which have preceded it.

For most minority communities, it is possible to identify three main strands in language reproduction: family, community and school. Responsibility for the transmission of minority languages in a British context began in the home. In the early days of post-war immigration, before there were any well-developed community activities, parents maintained the minority language and culture within the family.

Over a period of time, however, parents became anxious that their children were drifting away from traditional cultural and religious values. There was a gradual realisation that responsibility for language maintenance lay not only with the family but with the wider ethnocultural community and the first efforts to organise more formal language teaching were initiated. Hari Sewak Singh describes these early years of settlement for the Sikh community in Britain in the following terms:

> In the early days they were busy with buying houses and had other such preoccupations on their minds. They were not articulate enough to ask for mother tongue teaching in the school curriculum, and the communities were not yet well organised enough to arrange temple or mosque classes .... At the same time children were being strongly discouraged from using their mother tongues ... in language units and in schools.... At first Asian parents did not object to these attitudes and approaches in schools, for they recognised that English is commercially more valuable in the country in which they have chosen to live. However, when children grew into their teens, and started to lose the common language of the home, parents became more anxious. They could not follow the English of their teenage sons and daughters, and

there were many disputes... Many parents began openly to demand action within their own communities (Sewak, 1982, quoted in Edwards, 1983: 32)

Classes in languages such as Italian and Hebrew had been a feature of community life for many years. A marked increase in provision, however, took place in the late 1960s and early 1970s. In some cases, religious bodies have been an important force. The Catholic Church has played a key role in the teaching of Polish, Ukrainian and Lithuanian; mosques have fulfilled a similar role in the transmission of Qu'ranic Arabic and Urdu; and gurdwaras in the teaching of Panjabi. In other cases, the impetus and many of the resources came from the governments of the groups concerned. Thus, community language teaching in Italian, Spanish, Portuguese, Greek and Turkish is supported in varying degrees by the High Commission or Embassy in London.

Documentation on community language teaching in the early days of post-war immigration is extremely sparse. Community provision did not attract academic interest until the 1980s with the work of writers like Saifullah Khan (1980), Tsow (1984), LMP (1985), Taylor & Hegarty (1985), Taylor (1986), Bourne (1989) and Alladina & Edwards (1990). A catalyst for this scholarly attention was the debate arising from the Directive on the Education of the Children of Migrant Workers issued by the Council of the European Community (EC). A draft of the EC Directive, addressing the need for member states to teach the language and culture of migrants' children as part of the normal curriculum, was circulated to interested bodies in the UK in 1976. The response to proposals which had received little or no prior discussion among mainstream British educators was sometimes hostile. Teacher organisations objected on the grounds that expansion in this area was unacceptable in the face of educational cutbacks and teacher unemployment. The Government objected on various grounds including cost, difficulty in providing teachers and the inability of a decentralised education system to implement the Directive.

When the Directive finally appeared in July 1977, important modifications had been made. The revised document called upon member states to offer tuition only 'in accordance with their national circumstances and legal systems' and required them simply to 'promote' community language teaching. While considerable scepticism has been expressed about government willingness or ability to achieve even these modest aims (Bellin, 1980), the flurry of activity surrounding the Directive at least succeeded in placing community language teaching on the agenda of mainstream educators. Even so, the 1977 Directive has had considerably less impact on schools in Britain than on other member states. An EC report

(1984) on the implementation of the Directive provides interesting comparative data. For instance, just over 2% of UK children from linguistic minority communities are receiving 'mother tongue teaching' at school. This contrasts strongly with the situation in the Netherlands where there is provision for 80% of eligible children.

The Directive did, however, act as a catalyst for LEA recognition of community-run language classes. Sometimes this involved paying teachers' salaries, sometimes allowing rent-free accommodation and occasionally providing both salaries and accommodation. No national statistics are available, but the indications are that the number of classes and pupils involved in community language teaching is very large. The Directory of Mother Tongue Teaching (LMP, 1985), based on a survey undertaken in 1981/2, reports classes in 18 different languages for over 8,500 pupils in just three inner city LEAs. Yet, although LEA recognition for limited numbers of community language classes was widespread at the time of this survey, the majority of the classes received no LEA support.

Things have improved only slowly in the intervening years in spite of official support for community language teaching. The (1985) Swann Report recommended that LEAs should support language teaching in the community when this provision is contributing to the overall education of bilingual pupils by offering free accommodation in schools; by making grants for books and teaching materials; and by providing in- service courses and advice from the LEA advisory service. But, while Bourne (1989) reports that almost three quarters of LEAs responding to her survey 'were anxious to show that they made some provision to encourage pupils' development of their community languages', the main form of support remained free accommodation.

Community language teaching in schools

Despite the recommendation of the Swann report that language maintenance is the main responsibility of the minority communities themselves, there have been various attempts within mainstream education to give greater recognition to community languages. These developments have taken two main forms. First, schools can demonstrate a commitment to linguistic diversity by offering bilingual support and by developing resources and language awareness activities which acknowledge the multilingual composition of present day Britain. Activities of this kind have already been discussed in Chapter 5. Second, community languages can be introduced as a school subject. This course of action has much to recommend it, since the exclusion of community languages from mainstream education may have the effect of lowering their standing in the eyes of English-speaking and minority-language-speaking children alike. However, introduction into the regular curriculum has often been problematic.

Sometimes community languages are taught at the same time as high status subjects such as French or German and the take-up rate is low. Sometimes they are offered as an option against the so-called 'low status' subjects such as art, or sport, or in the lunch time or after school, rather than being integrated into the timetable. Bourne (1989), for instance, reports that a quarter of the LEAs responding to her survey provided resources for community language classes taking place after school hours. Although this kind of arrangement has the advantage of making it possible to provide teaching in languages spoken by smaller numbers of pupils, it risks reinforcing the low status of the languages on offer in schools. Sometimes community languages *are* integrated into the timetable but are taught in the same way as, for instance, French and German. This approach fails to recognise that, while the children concerned may not have native speaker proficiency, their understanding and productive abilities are well in advance of students learning a foreign language.

The first official recognition of the special challenges for community language teaching in schools comes in *Modern Foreign Languages for Ages 11 to 16* (DES, 1990a), which pays particular attention to the organisational aspects of teaching classes which may well include both native speakers of the target language and monolingual speakers of English:

> The inclusion of bilingual pupils in modern language classes inevitably broadens the range of language attainment that the teacher has to address. To respond to this range the teacher must take steps to provide opportunities for differential learning. Sometimes this will involve a menu of different activities. But often it entails presenting common themes and topics with suitably differentiated roles and follow-up tasks for pupils. A wider range of language attainment in this way makes demands on the teacher. But it also increases the teaching options. Through carefully structured peer group work it can increase opportunities for valid dialogue and facilitate the sort of interactive learning that is impossible if the teacher is the only significant live source and model of the target language (15.12).

The Swann Report recommended that community language teaching should come under the aegis of modern language teaching. Bourne (1989), however, reports a wide range of line managers in addition to modern languages advisers, including multicultural advisers, special services advisers and a humanities adviser. This often causes problems of communication, especially at secondary level. In addition, the fact that community languages continue to be excluded from modern languages guidelines and research projects (DES, 1986, 1988a) may well produce conflicts of interest. Modern language teachers may feel inclined to guard what they perceive to be their own territory and this may result in a neglect of community languages.

Another concern about the introduction of community language teaching is the amount of control which is exercised over what is taught. For most communities, language teaching cannot take place in isolation and must address the history, culture and religion of the people. The position currently taken by the government (DES, 1990a: 97) is that the teaching of a language should not be equated with the promotion of a particular religious or political viewpoint. This stance fails to recognise a major motivation for language transmission in minority communities. For this reason, members of the Polish community have resisted attempts to introduce Polish into the mainstream (Muir, 1990) and similar reservations have been expressed by the Chinese community (Wong, 1990). Various linguistic minority organisations have also expressed a great deal of concern about examination design. For instance, as a reaction against the public examination system, the Gujarati Literary Academy has developed a syllabus and textbooks for five graded examinations which place greater emphasis on cultural and literary heritage than mainstream syllabi (Dave, 1990).

The implementation of a National Curriculum in the wake of the 1988 Education Reform Act creates further problems for the teaching of community languages in the mainstream. In the primary sector, no provision has been made for the teaching of languages other than English and Welsh in Wales, and English in the rest of the UK. In the secondary sector, languages which can be taught were originally divided into two schedules. All schools were required to offer at least one of the eight working languages of the European Community which make up Schedule 1 languages. After this obligation had been fulfilled, schools could also offer a Schedule 2 language which included Arabic, Bengali, Gujarati, Hindi, Japanese, Mandarin or Cantonese Chinese, Modern Hebrew, Panjabi, Russian, Turkish or Urdu.

Criticism of the two list format and its implied hierarchy has led to the replacement of Schedules 1 and 2 with a single list of languages (DES, 1990a: 11.5) It might be argued, however, that this modification is largely cosmetic. The expectation remains that each pupil should be offered the chance to study a working language of the EC to meet the the National Curriculum foreign languages requirement. It is still the case that languages other than EC working languages can only be offered when the school already provides teaching in an EC working language.

The implicit message of these new arrangements is that the working languages of the EC are considered more important than Urdu or Panjabi or Cantonese. The Local Management of Schools (LMS), another radical change introduced as a part of the 1988 Education Reform Act, has given rise to widespread anxiety about the future of community language teaching. Given the low priority accorded to community language teaching in the National Curriculum, even those schools currently active in this area may find excuses to renege on their commitment, especially in those cases where education budgets have been reduced.

Heritage Language Teaching in Canada

The best known example of innovation in language teaching in Canada is almost certainly the French immersion education for English-speaking children. Various bilingual education programmes have also been set up for several different groups including Italian–English (Grande, 1975; Shapson & Purbhoo, 1977), Ukrainian–English (Lupul, 1976; Lamont et al., 1978) and French–English–Hebrew (Genesee et al., 1978). For the purposes of the present discussion, however, we will confine ourselves to situations where minority languages are the subject rather than the medium of education. Terminological confusion has surrounded the teaching of minority languages in Canada in much the same way as in the UK (Cummins & Danesi, 1990). However, since this area is now referred to consistently as 'heritage language teaching', it seems sensible to switch from 'community languages' to 'heritage languages' in discussing Canadian provision.

Whereas heritage language teaching in the UK has often met with indifference, antipathy and neglect on the part of the dominant wider society, this is an issue which has been more politically prominent in Canada. Until 1962, the immigration policy pursued by the Canadian government was essentially one of 'Whites only'. New legislation since this date, together with the need to compensate for falling birthrates, has resulted in important changes in the ethnic composition of the country. The Anglo-Celtic majority has been gradually eroded and has been increasingly forced to address the needs of much larger and more diverse ethnocultural communities.

Heritage languages have been a feature of Canadian life for many years, with a great deal of activity, for instance, in the Italian, Greek and Ukrainian communities, especially in the post-war period. The pressures of Anglo-conformity were such, however, that members of these communities were faced with only two real choices: either to assimilate to the dominant society or to make efforts to maintain the heritage language and culture within their own minority communities. The greater numbers and economic strength of linguistic minorities within Canada, however, created the possibility of an alternative response, as various different groups began to articulate the need for heritage language teaching to be recognised by the education system.

Heritage language teaching has, however, been a subject of public controversy and debate at federal, provincial and school board levels since the mid-1970s. Opinion has polarised around the question of whether diversity is a threat to Canadian society or whether differences in language and culture are a valuable resource. Opponents of diversity stress its socially divisive nature. They also argue that the promotion of diversity is very expensive and educationally unsound because, they claim, it detracts attention from the learning of English. Advocates of diversity, on the other hand, point to the benefits of bilingualism and multilingualism both for the individual and for society as a whole.

The strength of feeling is perhaps surprising, given the way in which Canadians have begun in recent years to project the notion of multiculturalism as characteristically Canadian. However, many commentators feel that, on closer examination, this popular view lacks depth. It can be argued, for instance, that the 'celebratory multiculturalism' (Cummins & Danesi, 1990) which is a feature of the highly acclaimed 'heritage weeks' in schools or St. Patrick's Day parades simply detracts attention from more pressing issues of equality and justice.

Despite the use of social and educational arguments, the debate remains essentially political. Although there are many important exceptions, heritage language teaching is, in general, opposed by the political Right and supported by the political Left. By the same token, the main opposition comes from the politically dominant English and French-speaking groups and the main support from the less politically influential ethnic minority groups. As Cummins & Danesi (1990: 22) point out:

> The primacy of political considerations in the heritage language debate obscures the fact that there is no educational reason why all Canadian children should not leave school at least trilingual; however, as a society we choose, for the most part, not to pursue this course because to do so would be to legitimise the knowledge, values and languages of ethnocultural groups who are still regarded as subordinate in Canadian society; the brittle remnants of Anglo-conformity would be further weakened by any intrusion of heritage languages into mainstream Canadian institutions'

Since the publication of the report of the Royal Commission on Bilingualism and Biculturalism in 1970, the official policy has been one of 'multiculturalism within a bilingual framework' in which there are two official languages – English and French – but no official culture so that no ethnic group takes precedence over any other. The very different demographic make-up of the Canadian provinces has produced a range of different emphases in the responses to the Royal Commission. For present purposes, however, discussion will focus on Ontario, partly because the bulk of the Canadian population and the highest numbers of ethnic minority communities are found in this province; and partly to provide a background for the analysis of heritage language teaching in the Ontario school board which forms a major focus for this study.

The initial response of the Ontario government and some of the larger school boards was to set up task forces and work groups on cultural diversity. At this point in the early 1970s, attention was paid to a range of issues including race relations, bias in textbooks, curriculum development for a multicultural society and heritage languages. It is highly significant that heritage language teaching was the only one of these issues which proved controversial.

The first challenge to the educational establishment was a proposal submitted to the Toronto School Board in 1972 for an Italian–English bilingual programme. Lind (1974: 48–9) reports that the New Canadian Committee which received the proposal 'went apoplectic' but finally accepted a radically modified submisssion for a kindergarten Italian programme. Other very limited programmes for the Chinese and Greek pupils were approved shortly afterwards. There was a lack of clear policy during this period and it is not difficult to see why some commentators (Lind, 1974; Cummins & Danesi, 1990) have described the Ministry of Education as trying, wherever possible, to avoid confrontation without actually doing a great deal.

The catalyst for public debate on heritage language teaching came in 1975 with the circulation of the draft report of the Toronto Board's work group on Multicultural Programs. The work group outlined a series of more positive responses to multiculturalism, including the suggestion that languages other than English and French should be used both as subjects and as languages of instruction; that existing bicultural–bilingual and transitional programmes should be expanded; and that third language subject credit courses should be introduced at secondary school level. The very negative media and public response to the draft report resulted in the presentation of a greatly modified final version in 1976. It argued, for instance, that because of the sharply divided opinion on the issue and the fact that Ministry policy was not going to change, no recommendation could be made with respect to third language teaching.

The demands for heritage language teaching from ethnic minority groups continued to gain momentum. In the absence of support from the Ministry of Education, the Italian government was providing funds for the teaching of Italian in the so-called 'Separate' or Catholic Schools which are administered independently. There was a growing realisation that, with the rapid expansion of the ethnic minority population in Ontario, 'interference' in this arena from other foreign governments was very likely. The Heritage Language Program was announced in 1977, close to provincial elections in which the ethnic vote was very important. Provision was made for two and a half hours a week of heritage language teaching which could take place at weekends, or as part of the regular school day extended by half an hour, or after school.

While the position of heritage languages had been greatly strengthened by both federal and provincial programmes, many ethnic minority communities, felt that there was room for a more imaginative response to language maintenance. The Armenians and Ukrainians in Toronto, for instance, were pressing throughout this period for the establishment of Alternative Language Schools in which heritage languages would not only be taught for half an hour a day but would be used also for school announcements and non-instructional conversation. In response to this pressure, a Work Group set up in 1980 recommended that wherever possible the heritage language programme should be gradually integrated into an extended school day; it also argued that the board should develop bilingual and trilingual programmes involving heritage languages.

Given the history of polarisation on this issue, it is not surprising that these recommendations proved highly controversial, with ethnic minority populations expressing their support and Anglo-Canadians bitter opposition. The implementation of the extended day option was approved for a small number of Toronto schools in 1983/4, subject to a community vote. Many teachers were very hostile to the changes and made their views clear to both students and parents. Members of the Toronto Teachers' Federation expressed their anger by working to rule for six months and threatening an all-out strike. Cummins & Danesi (1990: 41) suggest that the strength of this reaction cannot be explained in terms of the educational, financial and social arguments marshalled by opponents of the extended day, since there were already 30,000 students in integrated heritage language classes in the Separate School system at no cost to the taxpayer. There was no evidence that this programme had led to 'ghettoisation'; and there was no suggestion that it had given ri se to academic difficulties.

Further developments in the 1980s depended very much on the changing political balance of power, both locally and at provincial level. The

Toronto Board's right to implement the extended day was upheld by an arbitration report but, by this time, new school board elections had shifted the balance of power to the Conservatives. The new board took a 'softly, softly' approach: they made no changes to the integrated heritage language programme but they disbanded the School Community Relations Department which, among other aspects of its work, had been providing information to ethnic minority parents on heritage language issues.

The election of the Liberal party in Ontario in the mid-1980s, however, heralded sweeping changes in the political climate. Race relations and multiculturalism became a priority. Among early developments in this area was the publication in 1987 of a discussion document recommending that school boards would be required to provide classes in a language if 25 or more parents with children in the board requested it. It also stressed the need for curriculum development, dissemination of resources, teacher training and research. Although the document gave rise to the habitual public outcry on the part of Anglo-Canadians, the Ministry of Education went ahead and began implementing this policy in 1988/9. It is also perplexing to note that the Ontario Minister responsible for multiculturalism who, with the Minister of Education announced the new policy, voted against implementing such classes in the Scarborough Board of Education where he serves as a trustee (Edwards in press).

In spite of protests of this kind, heritage language classes have continued to thrive over the last decade. In 1977/78, for instance, 42 school boards were providing 2,000 classes in 30 different languages to 50,000 students. By 1986/7, an additional 30 boards were offering 4,364 classes in 58 different languages to 91,110 students (Canadian Ethnocultural Council, 1988). There were also a further 69,000 students attending 369 heritage language schools run by community groups which received funding from the federal Cultural Enrichment programme.

Some Common Concerns

The historical development of community/heritage language teaching has followed very different courses in Canada and the UK. Different political and demographic trends have resulted in quite different patterns of provision. The Canadian situation, at first sight, seems a great deal more favourable. The level of resourcing and extent of provision are impressive and official recognition of the importance of language maintenance would appear to be far less grudging. The fact remains, however, that despite differences in organisation and resourcing, teachers of minority languages in both countries face similar problems on a practical level. A number of issues occur again and again in both British and Canadian contexts, including the recruitment and status of community/heritage language teachers; the availability of in-service training; the suitability of teaching resources and methodologies; and the difficulty of relationships with mainstream teachers.

Recruitment and status of teachers

Teacher shortages are a serious problem in community language teaching in the UK (Bourne, 1989). One way around these shortages has been to employ on instuctor grade bilingual teachers holding overseas qualifications which are not recognised by the Department of Education and Science. However, the low pay, low status and lack of job security associated with the post of instructor is a source of widespread dissatisfaction for members of minority groups. There is clearly a responsibility for LEAs to tackle the problem of gaining Qualified Teacher Status (QTS) for bilingual staff. It is therefore a matter of some concern that little over half of LEAs in the Bourne survey reporting difficulties in recruiting bilingual teachers had attempted to gain QTS for minority teachers in the five years prior to the start of the survey.

The possibilities for initial training and retraining of bilingual teachers are extremely limited. Three primary and one secondary Post-Graduate Certificate in Education courses specialising in community language teaching were set up in co-operation with Local Authorities in the mid-1980s. The government has expressed support both for initiatives of this kind and also for more initial teacher training for ethnic minority students (DES, 1987). Some concern exists, however, as to the effect of concurrent changes in recruitment policy which limit the numbers of 'mature' students entering Higher Education after the age of 25. This change in policy will certainly make it more difficult to achieve the stated aim of attracting more ethnic minority teachers.

Nor is it likely that British born bilingual children will, in the course of time, relieve the teacher shortages. In one LEA reported by Bourne (1989), for instance, there were only two Urdu teachers. Any pupil wanting to specialise in this subject in preparation for entry to Higher Education, would have to cope with the real possibility that their teacher would not remain at the school for the duration of the two year A-level course. And in cases where the community language teacher is also a member of another department, such as Maths, there is very little likelihood of being able to replace a teacher with both subject and language teaching skills.

While problems of recruiting teachers from ethnic minority communities and questions of equivalence of qualifications remain high on the agenda of Canadian educators, the same issues do not arise in relation to heritage language teaching. By making heritage language provision outside the school day, it is possible for classes to qualify for provincial funding under the Continuing Education Program. Instructors do not need the Ontario Teachers' Certificate and can therefore be paid much less than Certified Teachers. The position of heritage language teachers in Canada is thus much closer to that of teachers in community-run classes in the UK than to that of mainstream community language teachers. The fact that, in the main, heritage language teaching is kept separate from the regular school programme thus raises questions concerning the marginal status of both heritage language teaching and heritage language teachers.

A radical solution to these problems has been proposed by Cummins (1991). He points out that, while some school boards provide heritage language teaching, first language assessment and school–home liaison, these functions are the responsibility of different individuals. He proposes instead that all three functions should be integrated and carried out by the same individual, ideally at the level of the local school:

> Thus the teaching of heritage languages would be seen as one aspect of the way in which the mainstream education system promotes equity and cultural understanding rather than being relegated to a marginal position outside of 'regular' schooling. By the same token, 'community language specialists' would carry out a legitimate and appreciated function within the mainstream educational system and have career ladders within this system.

Such a proposal neatly by-passes many of the problems associated with the current position of heritage language teachers. It also holds out interesting possibilities for community language teaching in British schools, which faces similar questions of marginalisation.

In-service training

Even when teachers are in post, there is evidence that they receive little support in adapting to school systems which are often very different from those which they have previously experienced. Teachers of community languages come from a wide range of backgrounds. Some will be qualified teachers working in mainstream education. Some will have worked in schools in their country of origin but never in Britain or Canada. The only qualification for the job of many others is that they themselves are bilingual and they will have received no professional training at all.

The diverse backgrounds of community/heritage languages teachers have important implications for the delivery of the curriculum. Staff who have been trained overseas often structure their teaching in a way which is markedly different from the relatively informal and child-centred approach of most British primary classrooms, or recent trends in modern language teaching (Muir, 1990; Husain, 1990), although there are some important exceptions to this trend (White, 1990). Sometimes the clash of teaching styles is too great for children to be able to cope with. Many community language teachers in the UK (see, for example, Papadaki d'Onofrio & Roussou, 1990) are particularly damning in their criticism of teachers seconded by an overseas government, whose lack of familiarity with the organisation of schools in the new country leads them to teach in ways which children sometimes find confusing or irrelevant.

Attention also needs to be given to the question of dialect differences (Danesi, 1986). How should the teacher of Bengali proceed in a class of children who, in the main, are speakers of Sylheti? Or in an Arabic class which serves a population of Moroccans who speak a variety far removed from either Qu'ranic or modern standard Arabic? *Modern Foreign Languages* (DES, 1990b: 97) suggests two principles which are in keeping with the prevailing attitudes towards non-standard dialects of English in the classroom:

(1) any knowledge of the target language which pupils bring into the classroom should be recognised, fully valued and built upon. Where these skills are in a regional or non-standard form of the language, the teaching approach should ensure that pupils appreciate the value placed on the languages of their homes and are not led to regard it as deficient or inferior;
(2) an important goal should be to teach and to develop proficiency in a standard form of the target language. Developing a proficiency in a standard language should be seen as an extension of their repertoire of communicative abilities, not as a replacement for 'incorrect' usage.

Attitudes towards non-standard varieties in other countries, however, are often just as negative as has traditionally been the case in Britain and it cannot automatically be assumed that community language teachers will be in sympathy with a 'repertoire' approach.

Against this background, the role of in-service training for teachers working in a new and rapidly developing field (DES, 1984b) is critical. There is a need for community language teachers to be informed of teaching styles and curriculum development in mainstream schools, and of recent advances in language teaching. There is also an urgent need to develop methodologies which address the different needs of community language teaching: approaches to modern language teaching assume no prior knowledge of the language, an assumption which clearly does not hold in the case of children studying the language of their ethnocultural community. Yet the level of fluency of these children is rarely on a par with native speakers of the language and it is clearly inappropriate to treat them as first language speakers. Despite the urgency of these needs, the availability of in-service for teachers is highly variable.

In the UK, there has been a variety of curriculum development projects in the area of linguistic diversity, including 'Language in the Multilingual Primary Classroom' and 'The Mother Tongue Project', both funded by the Schools Council; the Inner London Education Authority's 'Bilingual Under Fives' project; and an EC funded pilot project to develop community languages in the secondary curriculum (Broadbent, 1987). These projects have been firmly based on mainstream classroom practice. The fact that many community teachers are also involved in mainstream classes means that innovations in the mainstream inevitably have implications for those working in the community. The introduction of the new GCSE examinations for 16 year olds in 1986 also created a wide range of in-service opportunities for community language teachers. In-service stemming from initiatives other than these centralised projects has, however, been limited (Bourne, 1989), though growing numbers of community organisations, such as the Association for the Teaching of Gujarati and the Gujarati Literary Academy, have begun to provide their own training programmes (Dave, 1990). Many teachers also make their own arrangements for professional training, seeking, for example, places on the Royal Society of Arts diploma course on community languages.

In Ontario, there is also a wide range of in-service training. Yet despite the commitment of the Heritage Language Program to teacher training, this provision would appear to be poorly co-ordinated and to depend on the goodwill of teachers who often have little free time to spare for professional development. The supervisor of heritage languages for the Ferndale Board described the situation thus:

> Each board tends to have one big seminar a year. Some teachers go to seminars in more than one board. Of course, many teachers are working in the day time, so they can't study as much as they should. Also OISE [Ontario Institute for Studies in Education] gives a course each year. Again not many attend because they are working.

Various minority communities also organise their own seminars and conferences. The Chinese in Canada, for example, have a large annual national conference which attracts a great deal of attention. In addition to organised events of this kind, support is available from colleagues, both formally and informally. As a Hindi teacher in the Ferndale Board explained:

> If I have a problem I can call my subject leaders. Usually they give about two or three workshops a year. The last workshop I attended

was on games. We didn't talk, we just made games. We also had a
session on 'Whole Language' and I gave a workshop on puppetry.

It is hoped that the current commitment of the Government of Ontario
to heritage language teaching and the promise of funding for teacher
training will lead to a more structured approach to professional development. There has been some discussion of an Ontario Heritage Language
Teacher's Certificate in which organisations like the South Central Ontario
Heritage Language Association (SCHOLA) might take a central role. For
the time being, however, the situation is far from satisfactory and continues
to attract critical comment. Cummins & Danesi (1990) argue that the
absence of structures which would allow heritage language teachers to
obtain in-service training and accreditation for the teaching of heritage
languages is an example of institutionalised racism.

Appropriate teaching resources

There is a serious shortage of suitable teaching materials in both Canada
and Britain. Very often the content of the books and courses produced in
the home country fail to speak to the interests and experience of locally-
born children, and the linguistic level for a given age range is too advanced.
The result is that teachers are involved in a great deal of preparation, a very
time-consuming and often inefficient process which would be handled
more effectively on a more centralised level.

In the UK, materials development has been fairly haphazard. There have
been just two major initiatives targeted at the mainstream. At the primary
level, the ILEA, the EC and the Schools Council jointly sponsored the
Mother Tongue Project which began work in 1981. The aim was to produce
materials, initially in Greek and Bengali, which would help primary school
children develop skills in the community language alongside English
(Tansley, Nowaz & Roussou, 1985; Papadaki d'Onofrio & Roussou, 1990).
At the secondary level, the EC project (1984–7) on Community Languages
in the Secondary School Curriculum involved a team of teachers of Urdu,
Panjabi and Italian from mainstream schools. One aim was to produce
materials for the diverse situations and contexts encountered by community language teachers in the mainstream (Cervi, 1990). There have also
been a small number of local initiatives, some of which have been extremely effective. Bourne (1990), for instance, describes how one LEA
supported teacher secondments and drew on supplementary training
funds to produce a course in Urdu. The textbooks and other materials
which the team developed were made available for sale both within the
LEA and outside.

As we indicated in Chapter 5, there has been a marked growth in ethnic minority publishing in the UK. While community language teachers are still involved in a great deal of materials preparation, the greater availability of commercially produced publications better suited to the needs of British-born children has been a welcome development. In Canada, various materials tailored to the needs of children living in a North American setting are now available for the longer established linguistic minorities. For obvious reasons, more recently arrived ethnocultural groups do not have access to comparable resources. As a supervisory officer with responsibility for heritage languages commented:

> The Italian, Greek, Polish, Chinese and Ukrainian communities have been established for a long time. There are very solid community associations that have funding from several ministries for multilingual and multicultural activities. They produce textbooks and boards buy from them.

There remains, however, a serious shortage of teaching materials for more recently arrived groups, such as the Tamil, Panjabi or Urdu speakers.

Although there are signs of progress, materials development in both Canada and the UK is a continuing problem. There is a clear need in both countries for a more structured and centralised approach to materials production; there are also opportunities for international co-operation in this area. The small Ukrainian and Lithuanian communities in Britain, for example, make wide use of materials produced by their larger and well-organised North American counterparts (Jenkala, 1990; Boyd, 1990). By the same token, materials for the teaching of Urdu, Panjabi and Gujarati have been developed to a far greater extent in the UK than in Canada and, according to the teachers with whom we spoke, adapt well, in most cases, to the North American context.

The relationship of community and mainstream teachers

The Swann Report (1985) places the main responsibility for language maintenance on ethnic minority communities. It does, however, suggest that the presence of community classes on school premises might lead to mainstream teachers being better informed about their pupils' overall education. This optimism appears, in many cases, to be without foundation. Three of the schools studied in depth by Bourne (1989) provided accommodation for community language classes either after school or at the weekend. In one of these schools, the only contact was with the headteacher over administrative matters; a second had occasional contact through school events and assemblies. The third, however, presented a much more positive model of the kinds of benefits which can be achieved through close liaison. It had, for instance, established a 'community tea-cher' post for organising events and for liaison and had set up 'a com-munity room' for English classes for parents in the day, and after-school classes for children. Although the classes were organised by the local Sikh Temple, attendance was arranged through the school at the beginning of the school year. Close contact of this kind had made it possible to arrive at more satisfactory arrangements. For instance it was decided that first-year junior pupils (seven–eight year olds) should receive tuition in Panjabi within the school day to avoid fatigue.

Even this school, however, had not explored the full range of possi-bilities for co-operation with community classes. Many Inner London Schools have, for instance, taken seriously the suggestion in the Primary Language Record (Barrs et al., 1988) that the profiling of children's lan-guage development should deal with their development as a language user and not simply as an English-speaker. Such a profile needs to draw on the perceptions of the children themselves, their families and community language teachers, in addition to the experience of teachers in school.

The picture presented by Bourne (1989) is one of indifference and ignorance on the part of most mainstream teachers towards the activities of community classes. In contrast, the experience of those who are suffi-ciently interested to visit community classes is warmth, openness and great willingness to cultivate closer links with mainstream schools on equal terms. The same warmth and openness were experienced by the present writers in their contact with teachers of Panjabi, Farsi and Urdu in heritage language classes in the Ferndale Board. Yet, despite the greater resourcing and recognition of these classes, there was evidence of very similar tensions between heritage language and mainstream teachers.

Interviews with mainstream teachers made it clear that there was a great deal of ambivalence towards the heritage language programme. Some of the reservations were expressed on educational grounds:

> I have six year old kids who have been to school all day and then go to Panjabi school in the evening. These kids are too little to be at school all day and then have to sit at chairs and tables for that length of time. Maybe at that level it should be done in a play situation.

At other times, the arguments had a more overtly political bias and demonstrated a fundamental misunderstanding of the language learning process:

> One of the concerns that I hear from time to time is, 'Didn't they come to Canada? Why are they doing all this heritage language because basically they have to make a go of it over here.

Sometimes teachers felt unsure as to who should take responsibility for language maintenance. One Ukrainian teacher, for instance, reflected on her own confusion thus:

> Because I went to community classes myself, I felt more comfortable with the system where the community assumes responsibility for teaching your kids the language and the culture. By the same token, maybe it's healthy. The school my daughter went to sang the National Anthem in three languages. In Grade 8 she gave a speech in three languages. Maybe that's very good. Maybe I shouldn't feel uncomfortable.

Perhaps the most damaging aspect of the general uncertainty and ambivalence expressed by the mainstream teachers over heritage language teaching is the way in which these emotions developed into concerns over territoriality. In the words of one elementary school teacher:

> We've grumbled because the heritage language teachers take our staff room. They have classes in the staff room and the library. They leave bits of erasers and stuff all around. As teachers we have not held the highest opinion of these people in heritage languages and it's kind of sad. They don't teach in regular classes because it would be even more of a disturbance – we've got all our toys, activities, books... My gosh! We don't want anything wrecked. It's not an ideal situation for two different programmes to be sharing the same base.

This situation is, predictably, seen in rather different terms by those involved in heritage language teaching. For instance, the principal of the heritage language classes held in the same school as the teacher who made the previous comment had this to say on the same subject:

> I don't like the rooms here. I don't want to have a class on the stage. I don't want to use the lunch room. It's very hard for the regular day teachers to give up their room. They figure that when they die their room will be sealed behind them! It's very frustrating. I can appreciate the teacher's point of view: 'We spent three weeks doing this project, it could be wrecked'. I said to the teachers, 'That's what I'm here for. I see the room before the class come in, I see it when they leave. If there's any discrepancy, we'll get both parties together'. But they don't buy that.

It would seem that such territoriality is by no means restricted to this one school building. The supervisor of heritage languages for the Ferndale Board confirmed this picture of suspicion and mistrust. He cited the case of an irate school secretary phoning up on Monday to complain that items had been stolen from the school by heritage language students using the premises on the weekend. Further investigation revealed that the classes had been cancelled on the day in question. Nor did he feel that there was any justification for fears about damage to school property. He estimated that the bill for replacing missing or damaged items for the whole programme in the previous year had been in the region of $50.

The picture which emerges from our contact with the Ferndale Board where classes take place after school and at the weekend is one in which heritage language classes are seriously marginalised. By offering separate tuition, the message for students and teachers alike is that heritage languages are less important than subjects which form an integral part of the mainstream curriculum. Valuable opportunities are missed for exchanging information both on approaches to teaching and the progress of children, something which can hardly be in the best interests of minority children. Despite the greater level of funding and resourcing for Ontario heritage language programmes, the situation in Ferndale is, in many ways, just as unsatisfactory as it is in UK community language teaching.

This situation is neatly summarised in a report by British educators, Fox, Coles, Haddon & Munns (1987:20):

> Very impressive heritage language programmes, often well run and taught, disguise the fact that these languages are not actually a part of mainstream provision and can serve to marginalise the importance of the first language. School principals do not control them and some feel little ownership of them. Far from encouraging school to build upon the language and culture that the child brings from home, the programme can serve to encourage teachers to ignore it altogether as it is being dealt with by other agencies (quoted in Cummins & Danesi, 1990: 68).

Liaison between mainstream and heritage language teachers is not always a clear-cut matter. Demographic factors will sometimes mean that the students attending heritage language classes in a given school will come from far afield and the majority may be students at other schools in the day time. It is difficult in cases such as this to promote a sense of joint ownership or to discuss the progress of students. In many cases, however, there is a common population and the separation of heritage language teaching has the inevitable effect of cultivating an atmosphere of benign indifference. This is clearly illustrated in the remarks of the principal of a daytime school which shared a large proportion of the same students with the heritage language classes occupying the same premises:

> I haven't done anything to promote this. I haven't done anything to discourage it. I've just offered no leadership.

The present arrangements for heritage language teaching may be politically expedient in that they require little change and make few demands

of mainstream teachers. The fact remains, however, that such arrangements are not ideal in that they serve to perpetuate the lower status of
minority languages. Some commentators (e.g. Cummins & Danesi, 1990)
have pointed to the institutionalised racism which underlies this state of
affairs. Even within the present structures, a great deal of work remains to
be done in the areas of raising public consciousness and teacher education
if heritage language teaching is to emerge from its present marginal status.

Conclusion

Ethnic minority communities in Britain and Canada face quite different
political realities. Immigrants who have arrived in Canada since the 1960s
now represent a far larger proportion of the total population than their
British counterparts. In provinces such as Ontario and in cities such as
Toronto, the ethnic vote is so important that new Canadians are able to
assert their views on the educational needs of their children far more
effectively than has been the case in the UK.

The difference in the political power of ethnic minorities in the two
countries is a major contributory factor in the different patterns of provision for community/heritage language teaching. Nonetheless, there is
much common ground. In both cases, teachers come from a range of
professional backgrounds and often there is a mismatch between their
experiences and the expectations and delivery of mainstream educators.
In order to bridge this gap, in-service training and support are essential,
but in both Britain and North America, opportunities for in-service are
limited and take little account of teachers' other commitments. There are
also very few opportunities to encourage professional development in a
structured way.

Teachers in both countries share an urgent need for suitable teaching
materials and curriculum development. Materials and pedagogies need to
take into account the special situation of community/heritage language
students whose learning needs are quite different from those of students
of a foreign language. On a positive note, there would seem to be many
opportunities for co-operation between Canadian and British educators in
this area. Classes in Lithuanian and Ukrainian in the UK, for instance, draw
heavily on North American materials. Similarly, the well-developed resources for teaching Urdu and Panjabi and other south Asian languages in
Britain could easily be adapted to the Canadian situation.

Heritage/community language teachers in Canada and the UK also
experience the negative effects of ambivalent attitudes on the part of
mainstream educators. A range of attitudes, from indifference to hostility,
can be identified, the result of which is the loss of valuable opportunities

for collaboration in the education of bilingual children. Where herit-age/community language teaching takes place in isolation from the main-stream, there is the further problem of marginalisation. A great deal more attention needs to be devoted to structural issues of this kind and to ways in which institutional blockages can be removed.

There can be little doubt that the development of heritage/community languages teaching serves a vital role in legitimating minority languages. It is also clear that efforts to maintain minority languages are both natural and desirable, particularly those attempting to build bridges between first and subsequent generations in the early years of immigration. Given the formidable difficulties which face those involved in this area, however, the extent to which community/heritage language teaching can be seen to be a successful agent of language maintenance remains to be seen.

6 A Pause for Thought

The preceding chapters leave little doubt that local conditions in Canada and the UK are very different. The British education system is undergoing a period of rapid reform, with teacher attention focused firmly on issues such as the National Curriculum and the Local Management of Schools. Canadian schools are currently enjoying rather better material conditions, and teacher status and morale would seem a good deal higher. None the less, Canadian educators are dealing with problems peculiar to their own political and historical experience. The new policy of multiculturalism appears against a backcloth of negative attitudes towards French Canadians on the part of the Anglo-Celtic majority and a disrespect for the rights of native Canadians on the part of both French and English-speaking communities. The failure to ratify the Meech Lake Accord further emphasises national ambivalence about the changing composition of society and the implications of these changes for all aspects of social and educational policy.

Yet despite important differences, many common threads emerge from a comparison of British and Canadian education. We see a similar evolution in philosophical and political approaches to diversity in both countries. We can identify similar pedagogical concerns. We also see practical responses to shared challenges which are likely to have currency in both settings. In the closing pages of this report we pause for thought as we look at a range of issues which require urgent attention from researchers, policy makers and teachers.

Developments in the Post-War Period

The changes in educational policy and practice which have been outlined in the previous chapters are extremely wide-ranging. The initial reaction to immigrants and their children in both Canada and Britain was unmistakably assimilationist. Families were expected to abandon their home languages and cultures and to be absorbed into the dominant society. The low status and underachievement of ethnic minority groups was ascribed to their lack of fluency in English and their unfamiliarity with the 'British' or the 'Canadian way'.

Gradually, notions of assimilation gave way to a more liberal approach of cultural pluralism. Minority languages and cultures were seen no longer as a problem but as a resource. There was a growing understanding, too, that education for a multi-ethnic society should not be reserved for inner city schools. Teachers needed to prepare all children, Black and White, for life in a rapidly changing and increasingly interdependent world.

While representing an important step forward from assimilation, multi-culturalism has been criticised on the grounds that it is often tokenistic and fails to engage with the racism which is part of every day reality for large numbers of Black people. It has become increasingly clear that the celebration of diversity is not enough in itself to ensure racial equality in education. Far more fundamental issues, including the need for genuine community involvement in the life of the school, teacher expectations, streaming, the nature and content of assessment, schools' treatment of racist name calling and other aspects of racial harassment, need to be considered if teachers are serious about equality of educational outcome. In some quarters, multicultural education has begun to give way to anti-racist education.

Pedagogical Concerns

In parallel with developments in educational philosophy have come radical changes in theories of language teaching and new ideas on the most appropriate form of delivery of English as a second language. Traditionally ESL was seen as a specialist domain, offered as an intensive course to children in separate classes. The emphasis was on drilling structures in isolation rather than on more communicative approaches to language teaching. The research evidence and experimentation of the late 1970s, however, pointed firmly in a different direction. The mainstream class-room was seen as the most supportive environment for language learning. There, children in the process of learning English had access to a wide range of native speaker models and, when the classroom was organised in ways which encourage discussion and collaborative problem solving, many areas of the curriculum were seen to have enormous potential for language learning through active participation.

There was a growing awareness of the racist implications of separate provision which denied children access both to a full curriculum and to a wide range of English-speaking models. Separate provision raised other questions, too. When children needed to be bussed to special classes or centres, important teaching time was lost; uprooting children from their neighbourhood schools also had unfortunate social and psychological consequences. The realisation that the most appropriate place for children learning English was the mainstream classroom had implications both for teaching methodology and the role of the teacher. It was unthinkable that children should be left unsupported, to sink or swim in a traditional 'chalk and talk' classroom. In the transition to full integration, there was an urgent need for specialist teachers to plan with and work alongside the class or subject teacher. It also became clear that teachers working in this support role should not be seen as having sole responsibility for children in the process of learning English. Mainstream teachers needed to recognise their role in this process and to adapt their materials and classroom organisation so as to provide the best learning environment for *all* children.

The mainstreaming of bilingual learners has important implications not only for the learning of English as a second language but also for the educational experience of native English speakers. There are many opportunities for languages in addition to English to be introduced into the classroom in ways which enhance all children's 'knowledge about language' (DES, 1988a). The development of literacy skills in one language reinforces the development of these same skills in other languages. In the UK the presence of bilingual support teachers greatly facilitates this process. The encouragement of activities on other languages also presents monolingual children with a positive view of bilingualism. The chance to discuss different patterns of language use in multilingual classrooms – such as the style-shifting of monolinguals or the code-switching of bilinguals – helps deepen understanding of how language works.

The changing climate of opinion allows for other languages and dialects to be promoted alongside English as part of the total language repertoire of the class. It also makes it possible to find ways of teaching community/heritage languages more formally as part of the curriculum. The range of ways in which this is achieved varies both within and between Canada and Britain. In Canada, there is a great deal of federal and provincial support for heritage language teaching, most of which takes place outside of the regular school day. In Britain, official support for community language teaching is more limited, though there have been many interesting initiatives in teaching community languages to both ethnic minority and indigenous children.

Developments in this area clearly have resource implications. The availability of books which mirror the cultural diversity of the wider society has increased dramatically in the post-war period. There is a growing awareness of the dangers of stereotyping and importance of a critical approach towards the use of existing library stock. The range of children's books written in community languages for overseas audiences has rapidly increased in recent years, as, too have dual texts. Multilingual, multicultural audiovisual and play materials are more common. There have been developments, too, in resources which stimulate discussion of race and racism. Equally important, teachers are becoming more adept at developing their own resources. Yet while activity in this area is encouraging, materials which reflect a multicultural or anti-racist perspective still represent only a tiny proportion of the total stock in schools. There is also tremendous variation between schools and between individual teachers in levels of awareness of such issues.

The Need for In-Service

We have reached a point when many administrators and policy makers have either realised spontaneously or have been pressed to acknowledge that current provision often fails to meet the legitimate needs of minority pupils. There is widespread awareness of the extent of underachievement and an embryonic understanding of some of the structural and organisational aspects of school life which deny Black children access to equal opportunities. Racism has been acknowledged as a major problem in a wide range of official reports and also in the increasing numbers of policy statements on this question being issued by local education authorities and boards of education. Anti-racist education has finally made an appearance on the agenda. The formulation of race and education policies at a central level is quite clearly an important first step. However, the challenge which remains is the translation of policy into practice. How are individual schools and teachers to be persuaded of the need to make these policies their own? Questions of this kind are particularly pertinent in the UK where recent educational reforms have had the effect of marginalising activity in this area.

As we have seen, actual classroom practices often give rise to a great deal of concern. Teachers are sometimes intolerant of children's home languages and cultures and show limited understanding of the perceptions or the expectations of minority families. Even when a local education authority or board of education has developed a formal race and education policy, teachers often fail to understand its implications for their classroom practice. The prevalence of teachers who either subscribe to assimilationist views or who practise 'celebratory multiculturalism' has led to a compromise of the principles underlying the mainstreaming of children learning English. The widespread lack of understanding of the rationale for integration has led to an acceptance of practice which is often at odds with the official policy.

We have examined examples in Canada and in the UK of the headlong rush to implement a policy without the necessary investment in resources and in-service which would ensure a sounder understanding of the reasons for change and a greater willingness to adapt to recommended practice. The result is that current arrangements may sometimes be less satisfactory than the original provision which people sought to change. Since the mainstreaming of minority pupils tends to be a much cheaper option than the provision of specialist language classes, speculation that rapid change has been sanctioned for reasons of economic expediency cannot be dismissed. There is certainly evidence of a widespread lack of political will. Although the reforms which schools are being asked to implement are radical in nature and there are many competing demands on educational budgets, there can be no doubt that current policies could be implemented a great deal more effectively if the rhetoric of politicians was matched by an appropriate level of funding.

An interesting case in point is the development of a National Curriculum in the UK. Despite considerable teacher resistance, the government has largely succeeded in its wish to control centrally the content and, to some extent, the delivery of a National Curriculum. Although there has been criticism, for instance, of the lack of investment in staff training, the political will to effect change has been clearly demonstrated. The same cannot be said for the integration of second language learners in the mainstream.

A further complication in a UK context is the fact that in-service training no longer qualifies for Section 11 monies, the traditional source of funding for the education of children of New Commonwealth origin. This is a particularly regrettable state of affairs. The mainstreaming of second language learners has wide-ranging implications both for the retraining of class and subject teachers and for the professional development of support teachers in their new role. The new criteria for Section 11 funding are likely to marginalise still further the importance of in-service for education in diversity in schools which are often operating with reduced budgets.

However, given an adequate budget for development at the level of in-service and initial training, what kind of issues need to be addressed? Two main areas of development – the informational and the affective – must be addressed if educators are serious about change. There is, of course, an urgent need for accurate information on a number of questions which have implications for the multilingual, multicultural classroom. Which languages and dialects are spoken by the children? What are their religious backgrounds? What aspects of their life at home and in the community support their cultural life and their use of other languages? What constitutes normal bilingual development? What are the optimal conditions for learning second and subsequent languages? What are the implications of our current knowledge for assessment procedures and other aspects of classroom practice?

There is evidence that educators are very sensitive to questions of this kind. In an analysis of their in-service needs, principals, vice-principals and teachers at the Ferndale Board consistently identified issues relating to language and culture as a priority. There was also evidence of a desire for a 'programmatic' solution to teachers' problems. We received requests, for instance, for a checklist of things which teachers should and should not do. There would appear, however, to be rather less awareness of the need for personal development in more affective areas and the serious challenges which this creates on the level of individual teachers, schools and LEAs or school boards.

The awareness of the need for attitude change, however, is usually less well-developed. Schools in Canada and the UK have been faced with changing populations and changing circumstances and, typically, have reacted in a very *ad hoc* manner. There is ample evidence of the imperviousness of schools to demands for change of any kind (Taylor, 1986). Yet a necessary first step in providing an appropriate education for diversity is to acknowledge the widespread racism in society and to recognise that school is a microcosm of that wider society. As such it is essential to identify those structures, practices and expectations of the school which are racist in effect, if not in intent. Cummins (1988: 151) describes the challenges in the following terms:

> The task of changing basic attitudinal orientations is formidable and experience suggests that strong policy/legal provisions and incentives at the levels of Ministries of Education, universities and school boards are necessary. In addition, principals should make it clear that teachers with an Anglo-conformity orientation are out of place in their schools, and teachers should also communicate to other teachers that behavioural or attitudinal manifestations of institutionalised racism are unacceptable to them.

The position of Black teachers

One aspect of this institutionalised racism that schools continue to ignore at their peril is the position of Black teachers and the ways in which they have repeatedly been marginalised. Although LEAs and school boards in Canada and the UK complain that there are shortages of ethnic minority teachers, there has been little sign of a commitment to recruit from the pool of experienced Black teachers. There has been a widespread reluctance for instance, to recognise overseas qualifications and a failure to provide adequate opportunities for retraining. This policy of *laissez-faire* has several possible outcomes. Ethnic minority teaching candidates may decide to pursue an alternative career. They may enter teaching only to find that their prospects for career development are limited. Alternatively they may accept a post which is not commensurate with their potential or experience. The obstacles regularly encountered by Black teachers are summed up well by Hubah (1984: 30):

> Black teachers, like Black people in general, have always been at the bottom of the system – Scale 1 for 16 or 17 years; supply teachers; temporary terminal teachers; short contract teachers – these are all proof of the blatant discriminatory practices which we suffer.

The situation for teachers of English as a second language and community/heritage languages is particularly worrying. It is significant that the field of ESL is dominated in Canada and Britain by White monolingual teachers. As Hubah (1984: 28) points out:

> Asian teachers, for example, who are fluent in three or more languages and conversant with a number of dialects have applied for Scale posts as ESL or EFL teachers and have been turned down in favour of a White, Anglo-Saxon teacher often with little or no teaching experience. These Asian teachers are probably among the legions known to spend hours of their 'home time' translating into various languages – Bengali, Panjabi, Urdu, etc. – texts which are then used by White teachers who give no credit to the person whose linguistic skills made the work possible.

In the UK, additional pressures are likely to be caused by the changes in Section 11 funding already mentioned. Under the new rules, contracts will be issued for only three year periods, a situation which will make for a high degree of insecurity for teachers funded under Section 11, many of whom are Black. Because of financial implications of changes introduced in recent education legislation (Local Management of School) it will not be possible to ensure the redeployment of teachers made redundant by the disappearance of their Section 11 funded posts.

The discriminatory practices which exist in relation to the recruitment and professional development of Black teachers are a matter of grave concern, both in terms of social justice and in terms of wasted talent.

Whole school change

In-service can take many different forms. Individual teachers can go on courses provided by the LEA/school board or by an outside body. Groups of teachers from the same school can attend a course in the hope that what they learn will 'cascade' outwards to colleagues on their return to school.

Any in-service which does not focus directly on a given school will, however, confront a number of intractable problems. Courses designed and delivered by 'outside experts' may well fail to address local conditions or questions that teachers in a particular school have identified as their priorities. In addition, teachers returning from this kind of in-service may well feel marginalised and unable to implement the knowledge and ideas they have acquired.

A more viable alternative is to focus in-service on the school. There is evidence that educators in Britain and in Canada are moving increasingly towards this model of delivery. In many cases the foundation for whole school in-service is laid by providing initial training for key personnel. Senior management clearly play a critical role: they give an issue status by placing it on the agenda; they allocate resources; they disseminate information; they have responsibility for implementing board/LEA policy at the level of their school. In addition to senior managers, teachers with a known commitment to curriculum development in this area can usefully be singled out for initial training which will allow them to play an important role in in-service which then focuses specifically on the school.

In the UK, various developments, unrelated to cultural diversity, are reinforcing the trend towards whole school development. One of the achievements of the National Curriculum has been to focus teacher attention on 'the grand plan' and to encourage them to work together in defining and addressing common goals. Inconsistencies in approach between teachers and departments are confusing for children and frustrating for any teacher who welcomes the opportunity to discuss and deepen understanding of the issues. Whole school policies are becoming increasingly common on language across the curriculum (Corson, 1990), record-keeping and assessment (SEAC, 1990) and education for equality (CRE, 1988). The recently published Partnership Teaching materials for in-service (Bourne & McPake, 1991) capitalise on developments of this kind.

A school policy must, of course, be the result of collaborative effort. It is counterproductive to give one teacher the brief to produce a statement without extensive consultation and discussion with all colleagues. Policies produced in isolation will fill folders gathering dust on staff room shelves but fail to influence practice. Exploration and debate around an issue is ultimately more important for what happens in the classroom than the document which summarises this process. A policy can only become a working reality when teachers have the opportunity to make the underlying philosophy their own.

By the same token a school policy can never be a definitive statement of practice. We learn from experience and exposure to others who approach the same question in a different way. Any policy needs provision for monitoring and evaluation, with the expectation that there will be regular review. Policies formulated by other schools can serve as a useful starting point for discussion, but can never be taken on board as they stand. No two schools are alike. The experience, attitudes and backgrounds of individual teachers will vary enormously, as will the school population and existing practice.

Some Lessons Learnt

The opportunity to look closely at another education system is valuable in itself. It also offers scope for introspection. The similarities and differences observed in schools and structures in another country allow the visitor to focus more clearly on aspects of education in the home country which, all too often, are accepted without questioning. It seems appopriate to include at this point some personal observations on our experience as British researchers of talking to Canadian teachers, librarians, administrators, school board trustees, parents and community figures.

Our first impression was one of *déjà vu*. The anxieties frequently articulated in Canadian classrooms and staffrooms were all too reminiscent of our experiences in Britain. In many cases our feelings were ones of disappointment and dismay. Some of the sentiments expressed – 'Why don't they speak English if they come to this country?' 'I can't be expected to cope with non-English speakers in my classroom!' – pointed to a very limited understanding of the challenges associated with diversity in education. We had naively hoped that reservations frequently expressed in British staffrooms would not be reproduced in Canada.

On many occasions, however, we felt greatly encouraged by what we saw. Some teachers and a wide range of administrators and central support staff demonstrated a keen understanding of the issues and an ability to learn from other education systems that have faced similar challenges at different times. We were left with a feeling of the urgent need for contact between teachers, advisers/consultants, administrators and researchers in Britain, Canada and other countries attempting to provide education for diversity. The chance to discuss and share is vital if we are to learn from mistakes already made, or to benefit from fresh perspectives on similar problems.

The realisation that the same issues recurred with startling regularity in both contexts also underlined the scale of the challenge facing schools. The rhetoric is now in place: school boards/LEAs and politicans are, for the most part, commmitted to the notion of racial equality in education. A great deal more needs to be done, however, in recognising and eradicating the

structural and attitudinal blocks which stand in the way of equal opportunities. And unless there is the political will to divert considerably more
funding to developments in this area, the many race and education policies
produced in recent years will simply not be worth the paper they are
written on.

Which Metaphor?

One of the major obstacles to real development is the prevalence of two
widespread and very similar myths which cloud the understanding of
White middle class teachers as to the issues which systematically place
minority pupils at a disadvantage. In the UK, this myth takes the form of
British 'fair play'. In spite of our colonial history and the overwhelming
evidence of racism at all levels in society, many people continue to believe
that we live in a basically just society. In Canada, the notion of the 'cultural
mosaic' or 'the salad bowl' serves a very similar function in defining a
national identity with which the dominant group can feel comfortable.

It seems to us, however, that the situation in Canada, as indeed in the
UK, is far too complex to be encapsulated in metaphors of this kind,
however enticing they may be. Current provision sends out mixed messages to all children – Black and White. Canadian and British teachers share
a similar range of bigotry and racism. They also cherish the same hopes
and aspirations for a more just society which offers genuine equality of
educational opportunity and outcome. The challenge for educators in both
countries is to find ways of acknowledging, recognising and erasing the
racism which exists on the level of the individual and the institution and
to press for the political will to resource developments on a realistic scale.

References

Alladina, S. and Edwards, V. (1990) *Multilingualism in the British Isles,* 2 vols. London: Longman.

Antonouris, G. and Wilson, J. (1988) *Equal Opportunities in School: New Dimensions in Topic Work.* London: Cassell.

Bagley, C. (1986) Multiculturalism, class and ideology: A European–Canadian comparison. In S. Modgil, G. Verma, R. Mallick and C. Modgil (eds) *Multicultural Education: The Interminable Debate* (pp. 49–59). London: Falmer Press.

Bakhsh, Q. and Walker, N. (1980) *Unrealised Potential. Gravesend Study. The Case for Additional Resources Under Section 11.* Gravesend: Gravesend and District Community Relations Council.

Barrs, M., Ellis, S., Hester, H. and Thomas, A. (1988) *The Primary Language Record Handbook for Teachers.* London: Inner London Education Authority, Centre for Language and Primary Education.

— (1990) *Patterns of Learning: The Primary Language Record and the National Curriculum.* London: Inner London Education Authority, Centre for Language and Primary Education.

Bellin, W. (1980) The EEC Directive on the Education of the Children of Migrant Workers: a comparison of the Commission's proposed Directive and the Council Directive together with a parallel text. *Polyglot* 2, Fiche 3.

Bernstein, B. (1970) *Class, Codes and Control* Volume 1. London: Routledge.

Berry, J., Kalin, R. and Taylor, D. (1977) *Multiculturalism and Ethnic Attitudes in Canada.* Ottawa: Ministry of Supply and Services Canada.

Bissonnette, L. (1989) School boards' ugly idea pushed back into hiding. *Globe and Mail* 25 November.

Black, N. (1913) *English for the Non-English.* Regina: Regina Book Shop Ltd.

Bourne, J. (1989) *Moving into the Mainstream: LEA Provision for Bilingual Pupils.* Windsor: NFER/Nelson.

Bourne, J. and Cameron, D. (1988) No common ground: Kingman, grammar and the nation. *Language and Education* 2(3), 147–60.

Bourne, J. and McPake, J. (1991) *Partnership Teaching: Co-operative Teaching Strategies for English Language Support in Multilingual Classrooms.* London: HMSO.

Boyd, J. (1990) The Lithuanian speech community. In S. Alladina and V. Edwards (eds), Vol. 1, pp. 136–142.

Brah, A. and Minhas, R. (1988) Structural racism or cultural difference: Schooling for Asian girls. In M. Woodhouse and A. McGrath (eds) *Family, School and Society* (pp. 215–22). London: Hodder and Stoughton.

Brandt, G. (1986) *The Realization of Anti-Racist Teaching.* London: Falmer Press.

Breton, R. (1986) Multiculturalism and Canadian nationbuilding. In A. Cairns and C. Williams (eds) *The Politics of Gender, Ethnicity and Language in Canada* (pp. 27–66). Toronto: University of Toronto Press.

Breton, R., Reitz, J., and Valentine, V. (1980) *Cultural Boundaries and the Cohesion of Canada.* Montreal: Institute for Research on Public Policy.

Brière, E. (1973) Cross-cultural biases in language testing. In J. Oller and J. Richards (eds) *Focus on the Learner: Pragmatic Perspectives for the Language Teacher* (pp. 214–27). Rowley, Mass; Newbury House.

Broadbent, J. (1987) *The Inclusion of Community Languages in the Normal Curricular Arrangements of LEA Maintained Schools in England and Wales.* London: University of London Institute of Education.

Brown, C. (1984) *Black and White Britain: The Third PSI Survey.* London: Heinemann.

Bullock, Sir A. (1975) *A Language for Life.* London: HMSO.

Burnet, J. (1984) Myths and multiculturalism. In R. Samuda *et al.* (eds) *Multiculturalism in Canada: Social and Educational Implications.* Boston: Allyn and Bacon.

Campos, S.J. and Keatinge, R. (1988) The Carpinteria language minority student experience: From theory, to practice, to success. In J. Cummins and T. Skutnabb-Kangas (eds) *Minority Education: From Shame to Struggle* (pp. 299–307). Clevedon, Avon: Multilingual Matters.

Carby, H. (1980) Multicultural fictions. Occasional Stencilled Paper No. 58, Centre for Contemporary Cultural Studies, University of Birmingham.

Canadian Ethnocultural Council (1988) *The Other Candian Languages: A Report on the Status of Heritage Languages Across Canada.* Ottowa: Canadian Ethnocultural Council.

Cartwright, D. (1988) Language policy and internal geopolitics. In C. Williams (ed.) *Language in Geographic Context.* Clevedon, Avon: Multilingual Matters.

Cashmore, E. (1982) *Black Sportsmen.* London: Routledge and Kegan Paul.

Cervi, B. (1990) The Italian speech community. In S. Alladina and V. Edwards (eds), Vol. 1, pp. 214–27.

Chatwin, R. (1985) Can ESL teaching be racist? In C. Brumfit *et al.* (eds) pp. 181–6.

— (1990) Assessing national assessment: How should we respond? *Multicultural Education Review* 10, 3–8.

Clark, R., Fairclough, N. Ivanic, R. and Martin-Jones, M. (1991) Critical language awareness: Towards critical alternatives. *Language and Education* 5(1), 41–54.

Coard, B. (1971) *How the West Indian Child is Made Educationally Sub-Normal in the British School System.* London: New Beacon Books.

Commission for Racial Equality (CRE) (1986) *The Teaching of English as a Second Language.* London: HMSO.

— (1988) *Learning in Terror: A Survey of Racial Harassment in Schools and Colleges.* London: HMSO.

Corson, D. (1990) *Language Policy Across the Curriculum.* Clevedon, Avon: Multilingual Matters.

Craft, A. and Klein, G. (1986) *Agenda for Multicultural Teaching.* SCDC, York: Longman.

Cummins, J. (1983) *Heritage Language Education: A Literature Review.* Toronto: Ontario Ministry of Education.

— (1984) *Bilingualism and Special Education: Issues in Assessment and Pedagogy.* Clevedon, Avon: Multilingual Matters.

— (1988) From multiculturalism to anti-racist education. In T. Skutnabb-Kangas and J. Cummins (eds) *Minority Education: From Shame to Struggle* (pp. 127–57). Clevedon, Avon: Multilingual Matters.

— (1991) Personal communication.

Cummins, J. and Bountrogianni, M. (1986) Assessment of minority children. In T.V. Ontario (ed.) *Educating the Special Child: Viewers' Guide* (pp. 40–3). Toronto: TV Ontario.

Cummins, J. and Danesi, M. (1990) *Heritage Languages: The Development and Denial of Canada's Linguistic Resources.* Toronto: Our Schools/Ourselves Education Foundation and Garamond Press.

Cummins, J. and Troper, H. (1985) Multiculturalism and language policy in Canada. In J. Cobarrubias (ed.) *Language Policy in Canada: Current Issues.* Québec: CIRB/ICRB.

Danesi, M. (1986) *Teaching a Heritage Language to Dialect-Speaking Students.* Toronto: OISE Press.

Daniel, W. (1968) *Racial Discrimination in England.* Harmondsworth: Penguin.

Darcy, N. (1953) A review of the literature on the effects of bilingualism upon the measurement of intelligence. *Journal of Genetic Psychology* 82, 21–57.

Dave, J. (1990) The Gujarati speech community. In S. Alladina and V. Edwards (eds), Vol. 2, pp. 88–102.

Delamont, S. and Galton, M. (1986) *Inside the Secondary Classroom.* London: Routledge & Kegan Paul.

Deosoran, R. (1976) *The Every Student Survey.* Toronto: The Board of Education for the City of Toronto.

Department of Education and Science (DES)(1970) *Statistics of Education.* London: HMSO.

— (1971) *The Education of Immigrants.* Education Survey 13. London: HMSO.

— (1972) *The Continuing Needs of Immigrants.* Education Survey 14. London: HMSO.

— (1984a) *English from 5 to 16.* London: HMSO.

— (1984b) *Mother Tongue Teaching in School and Community: An HMI Inquiry in 4 LEAs.* London: HMSO.

— (1986a) *English from 5 to 16: The Responses.* London: HMSO.

— (1986b) *Foreign Languages in the School Curriculum.* London: HMSO.

— (1987) *Draft Circular on Ethnically-based Statistics on School Teachers.* London: DES.

— (1988a) *Report of the Committee of Inquiry into the Teaching of the English Language* (The Kingman Report). London: HMSO.

— (1988b) *A Survey of the Teaching of English as a Second Language in Six LEAs.* London: DES.

— (1988c) *Task Group on Assessment and Testing: A Report.* London: HMSO.

— (1989) *English for Ages 5 to 16* (The Cox Report). London: HMSO.

— (1990a) *Teaching Modern Foreign Languages for Ages 11–16.* London: HMSO.

— (1990b) *National Curriculum Assessments: Statutory Instruments.* London: HMSO.

Dixon, B. (1977) *Catching Them Young.* 2 vols. London: Pluto.

Donmall, G. (ed.) (1985) *Language Awareness.* London: National Congress on Languages in Education.

Dulay, H., Burt, M. and Krashen, S. (1982) *Language Two*. New York: Oxford University Press.

Dummett, A. and Martin, I. (1982) *British Nationality: The AGIN Guide to the New Law*. London: Action Group on Immigration and Nationality/National Council for Civil Liberties.

Edwards, J. (1989) *Language and Disadvantage* (2nd edn). London: Cole and Whurr.

— (1992) Ethnolinguistic Pluralism and its discontents: A Canadian study and some general observations. *International Journal of the Sociology of Language*.

— (in press) Identity and language in the Canadian educational context. In K. McLeod, S. Cipywnyk-Morris and M. Danesi (eds) *Heritage Languages and Education: Language and Learning*.

Edwards, V. (1983) *Language in Multicultural Classrooms*. London: Batsford.

— (1986) *Language in a Black Community*. Clevedon, Avon: Multilingual Matters.

Edwards, V., Goodwin, J. and Wellings, A. (eds) (1991) *English 7–14: Every Child's Entitlement*. London: David Fulton.

Edwards, V. and Redfern, A. (1988) *At Home in School: Parent Participation in Primary Schools*. London: Routledge.

Esling, J. (ed.) (1989) *Multicultural Education and Policy in the 1990s*. Toronto: OISE Press

European Communities (EC)(1977) *Council Directive on the Education of Children of Migrant Workers: 77.486*. Brussels: EC.

— (1984) *Report on the Implementation of Directive 77/486/EEC on the Education of Children of Migrant Workers*. Brussels: EC.

Fathman, A. (1976) Variables affecting the successful learning of English as a second language. *TESOL Quarterly* 10(4), 433–41.

Fish, J. (1985) *Educational Opportunities for All?* London: Inner London Educational Authority.

Fitzpatrick, B. (1987) *The Open Door*. Clevedon, Avon: Multilingual Matters.

Flew, A. (1987) *Power to the Parents*. London: Sherwood Press.

Foster, M. (1982) Indigenous languages in Canada. *Language and Society (Ottowa)* 7, 20–4.

Fox, J., Coles, M., Haddon, S. and Munns, R. (1987) Study visit to Toronto. Multi-cultural Education. Unpublished report.

Friesen, J. (1987) Multicultural policy and practice: What about the Indians? *Journal of Native Education* 14(1), 30–40.

Fuller, M. (1983) Qualified criticism: critical qualifications. In L. Barton and S. Walker (eds) *Race, Class and Education* (pp. 166–90). Beckenham: Croom Helm.

Galton, M., Simon, B. and Croll, P. (1980) *Inside the Primary Classroom*. London: Routledge and Kegan Paul.

Genessee, F., Lambert, W. and Tucker, G. (1978) An experiment in trilingual education. *Language Learning* 28, 343–65.

Gipps, C. (1990) *Assessment: A Teacher's Guide to the Issues*. London: Hodder & Stoughton.

Gipps, C., Steadman, S. Blackstone, T. and Stierer, B. (1983) *Testing Children: Standardized Testing in Local Education Authorities and Schools*. London: Heinemann.

Goodwin, J. and Wellings, A. (1991) They don't have any Black people in the book. In V. Edwards, J. Goodwin and A. Welllings (eds) *English 7–14: Every Child's Entitlement* (pp. 70–82). London: David Fulton.

Gram, P. (1988) What the letter from No. 10 said. *Times Educational Supplement* March 18th.

Grande, A. (1975) A transitional program for young immigrant children. In A. Wolfgang (ed.) *Education of Immigrant Students* (pp. 81–98). Toronto: Ontario Institute for Studies in Education.

Grinter, R. (1985) Bridging the gulf: The need for anti-racist multicultural teaching. *MulticulturalTeaching* 3(2).

Hale, T. and Burdar, E. (1970) Are TESOL classes the only answer? *Modern Languages Journal* LIX, 15–18.

Hamers, J. and Blanc, M. (1989) *Bilinguality and Bilingualism*. Cambridge: Cambridge University Press.

Handscombe, J. (1989) Mainstreaming: Who needs it? In J.Esling (ed.) *Multicultural Education and Policy in the 1990s* (pp. 18–35). Toronto: OISE Press.

Hargreaves, D. (1984) *Improving Secondary Schools: Report*. London: Inner London Education Authority.

Hart, S. (1986) Evaluating support teaching. *Gnosis* 9.

Hatcher, R. (1990) Newsfile—Section X1. *Multicultural Teaching* 9 (1), 34.

Hawkins, E. (1984) *Awareness of Language*. Cambridge: Cambridge University Press.

Hegarty, S. and Lucas, D. (1978) *Able to Learn? The Pursuit of Culture-Fair Assessment*. Windsor: National Foundation for Educational Research.

Her Majestys Stationery Office (HMSO) (1981) *Racial Attitudes*. London: HMSO.

Hessari, R. and Hill, D. (1989) *Practical Ideas for Multicultural Learning and Teaching in the Primary Classroom*. London: Routledge.

Hodges, L. (1990) National Crisis. *Education* May 18th.

Houlton, D. (1985) *All Our Languages. A Handbook for the Multilingual Classroom*. London: Edwards Arnold.

Houlton, D. and Willey, R. (1983) *Supporting Children's Bilingualism*. London: Longman for the Schools Council.

Hubah, L. (1984) The position of Black teachers in this society. In *All London Teachers Against Racism and Fascism (1984): Challenging Racism* (pp. 25–47). London: ALTARF.

Hughes, D. and Kallen, E. (1974) *The Anatomy of Racism: Canadian Dimensions*. Montreal: Harvest House.

House of Commons (1984) *Equality Now*. Ottawa: Canadian Government Publishing Centre.

Husain, J. (1990) The Bengali speech community. In S. Alladina and V. Edwards (eds), Vol. 2, pp.75–87.

Inner London Education Authority (ILEA) (1987) *Language Census*. London: ILEA Research and Statistics.

Jenkala, M. (1990) The Ukrainian speech community. In S. Alladina and V. Edwards (eds), Vol. 1, pp. 157–69.

Johnson, D. (1984) *Deadly Ending Season*. London: Karia Press.

Johnson, L.K. (1981) *Inglan is a Bitch*. London: Race Today Publications.

Jones, A.P. (1989) Language awareness in British schools. In J. Cheshire, V. Edwards, H. Münstermann and B. Weltens (eds) *Dialect and Education: Some European Perspectives* (pp. 269–81). Clevedon, Avon: Multilingual Matters.

Kalbach, W. (1979) Immigration and population change. *TESL Talk* 10, 16–31.

Khan, T. and Siddiqui, W. (1988) *Urdu Boliye*. London: BBC School Radio Productions.

Klein, G. (1985) *Reading into Racism*. London: Routledge and Kegan Paul.

Labov, W. (1982) Objectivity and commitment in linguistic science: The case of the Black English trial in Ann Arbor. *Language in Society* 11, 165–201.

Lamont, D., Penner, W., Blowers, T., Mosychuk, H and Jones, J. (1978) Evaluation of the second year of a bilingual (English–Ukrainian) program. *Canadian Modern Language Review* 34, 175–85.

Laycock, L. (1989) *Testing Reading: An Investigation*. London: Centre for Language in Primary Education.

Leaman, O. and Carrington, B. (1985) Athleticism and the reproduction of gender and ethnic marginality. *Leisure Studies* 4, 214.

Lewis, R. (1988) *Anti-Racism: A Mania Exposed*. London: Quartet.

Levine, J. (1981) Developing new pedagogies for multilingual classes. *English in Education* 15(3), 25–33.

— (ed.)(1990a) *Bilingual Pupils and the Mainstream Curriculum*. London: Falmer.

— (1990b) An historical perspective 1960s–1980s. In J.Levine ed.) (1990a), pp. 11–26.

Lind, L. (1974) *The Learning Machine: A Hard Look at Toronto Schools*. Toronto: Anansi.

Linguistic Minorities Project (LMP)(1985) *The Other Languages of England*. London: Routledge.

Lupul, M. (1976) Bilingual education and the Ukrainians in Western Canada: Possibilities and problems. In M. Swain (ed.) *Bilingualism in Canadian Education: Issues and Research*. Edmonton: Canadian Society for the Study of Education.

— (1981) Bilingual education and the Ukrainians in Western Canada: Possibilities and problems. In M. Swain (ed.) *Bilingualism in Canadian Education: Issues and Research*. Edmonton: Canadian Society for the Study of Education.

Mallea, J. (1989) *Schooling in Plural Canada*. Clevedon, Avon: Multilingual Matters.

Martin-Jones, M. and Saxena, M. (1990) Developing a partnership with bilingual classroom assistants. University of Lancaster ESRC Project Bilingual Resources in Primary Classroom Interaction, Working Paper 1.

Massey, I. (1991) *More than Skin Deep: Developing Anti-Racist Multicultural Education in School*. Sevenoaks, Kent: Hodder and Stoughton.

Mercer, L. (1981) Ethnicity and the supplementary school. In N. Mercer (ed.) *Language in School and Community* (pp. 147–60). London: Edward Arnold.

Milner, D. (1983) *Children and Race: Ten Years On*. London: Ward Lock Educational.

Ministry of Education (1963) *English for Immigrants*. London: HMSO 1963.

Moghaddam, F. and Taylor, D. (1987) The meaning of multiculturalism for visible minority immigrant women. *Canadian Journal of Behavioural Science* 19, 121–36.

Mortimore, P., Sammons, P., Stoll, L., Lewis D. and Ecob, R. (1988) *School Matters: The Junior Years*. London: Open Books.

Muir, E. (1990) The Polish speech community. In S. Alladina and V. Edwards (eds), Vol. 1, pp.143–56.

Mullard, C. (1982) Multiracial education in Britain: From assimilation to cultural pluralism. In J. Tierney (ed.) *Race, Migration and Schooling* (pp. 120–33). Eastbourne: Holt, Rinehart and Winston.

— (1984) *Anti-Racist Education and the 3Rs*. London: National Association for Multiracial Education.

Multiculturaliam and Citizenship Canada (1988) *Access to Education in a Multicultural Society*. Ottowa: Ministry of Supply and Services.

Nicholas, J. (1988) British language diversity surveys (1977–1987): A critical examination. *Language and Education* 2 (1), 14–33.

— (1989) Breaking the spiral of silence: An examination of the after effects of language diversity surveying in a British College of Further Education. *Language and Education* 3 (3), 183–208.

O'Bryan, K., Reitz, J. and Kuplowska, O. (1976) *Non-official Languages*. Ottowa: Ministry of Supply and Services Canada.

Ontario Ministry of Education (1988) *English as a Second Language and English Skills Development. Intermediate and Senior Divisions*. Toronto: Ontario Ministry of Education.

Papadaki d'Onofrio, E. and Roussou, M. (1990) The Greek speech community. In S. Alladina and V. Edwards (eds), Vol. 1, pp. 189–212.

Peal, E. and Lambert, W. (1962) The relation of bilingualism to intelligence. *Psychological Monographs* 76, 546.

Picard, A. (1989) Montreal school survey on 'ethnics' assailed. *Globe and Mail* 11 November.

Plowden, B. (1967) *Children and their Primary Schools*. London: HMSO.

Pollack, M. (1972) *Today's Three Year Olds in London*. London: Heinemann.

Porter, J. (1965) *The Vertical Mosaic: An Analysis of Social Class and Power in Canada*. Toronto: University of Toronto Press.

— (1972) Dilemmas and contradictions of a multi-ethnic society. *Transactions of the Royal Society of Canada* 10, 193–205.

— (1979) *The Measure of Candian Society*. Toronto: Gage.

Preiswerk, R. (1980) *Racism in Children's Books*. Geneva: World Council of Churches.

Pye, E. (1991) Media education. In V. Edwards, J. Goodwin, and A. Wellings (eds) *English 7–14: Every Child's Entitlement* pp. 61–8). London: David Fulton.

Rampton, A. (1981) *West Indian Children in Our Schools* (Interim Report of the Committee of Inquiry into the Education of Children from Ethnic Minority Groups). London: HMSO.

Redfern, A. and Edwards, V. (1991) Oracy. In V. Edwards, J. Goodwin, and A. Wellings (eds) *English 7–14: Every Child's Entitlement* (pp. 6–24). London: David Fulton.

Reid, E. (1988) Linguistic minorities and language education: The English experience. *Journal of Multilingual and Multicultural Development* 9 (1/2), 181–92.

Richardson, R. (1982) Talking about equality: The use and importance of discussion in multicultural education. *Cambridge Journal of Education* 12 (2), 101–14.

Riley, S. and Bleach, J. (1985) Three moves in the initiating of mainstreaming at secondary level. In C. Brumfit, R. Ellis and J. Levine (eds) (1985) *English as a Second Language in the United Kingdom* (pp. 77–90). Oxford: Pergamon.

Royal Commission on Bilingualism and Biculturalism (1966) *Preliminary Report.* Ottowa: Ministry of Supply and Services Canada.

— (1970) *Book IV. The Cultural Contribution of the Other Ethnic Groups.* Ottowa: Ministry of Supply and Services Canada.

Saifullah Khan, V. (1980) The mother-tongue of linguistic minorities in multicultural England. *Journal of Multilingual and Multicultural Development* 1 (1): 71–88.

Samuda, R. (1979) How are the schools of Ontario coping with a New Canadian population: A report of recent research findings. *TESL Talk* 11, 44–51.

— (1986) The Canadian brand of multiculturalism: The myth of multiracial education. In S. Modgil, G. Verma, R. Mallick and C. Modgil (eds) *Multicultural Education: The Interminable Debate* (pp. 101–9). Lewes: Falmer Press.

Samuda, R.J. and Crawford, D.H. (1980) *Testing, Assessment, Counselling and Placement of Ethnic Minority Students.* Toronto: Ontario Ministry of Education.

Schools Council (1967) *English for the Children of Immigrants.* Working Paper 13. London: HMSO.

— (1982) *Multicultural Education.* London: Schools Council.

Sewak, H. (1982) Mother tongue: The importance of Asian languages in Britain. In *Talking and Telling* (pp. 67–9). Reading: Language and Intercultural Support Service.

Shapson, S. and Purbhoo, M. (1977) A transition program for Italian children. *Canadian Modern Language Review* 33, 486–96.

Shaw, J. (1983) Gaelic revisited: Maintaining Gaelic in Cape Breton in the 80s. In J. Cummins (ed.) *Heritage Language Education: Issues and Directions.* Ottawa: Multiculturalism Canada.

Skutnabb-Kangas, T. and Cummins, J. (eds) (1988) *Minority Education: From Shame to Struggle.* Clevedon, Avon: Multilingual Matters.

Smith, D. (1977) *Racial Disadvantage in Britain.* Harmondsworth: Penguin.

Smith, D, and Tomlinson, S. (1989) *The School Effect: A Study of Multiracial Comprehensives.* London: Policy Studies Institute.

Solomon, P. (1988) Black cultural forms in schools: A cross national comparison. In L. Weis (ed.) *Class, Race and Gender in American Education* (pp. 249–65). New York: State University of New York Press.

— (1989) Dropping out of academics: Black youth and the sports sub- culture in a cross-national perspective. In L. Weis, E. Farrar and H. Petrie (eds) *Dropouts From School: Issues, Dilemmas and Solutions* (pp. 79–93).

Stenhouse, L. (1975) *An Introduction to Curriculum Research and Development.* London: Heinemann.

Stone, M. (1981) *The Education of the Black Child in Britain: The Myth of Multicultural Education.* London: Fontana.

Stubbs, M. (1989) The state of English in the English state: Reflections on the Cox Report. *Language and Education* 3 (4), 235–50.

Surkes, S. (1989) Test monster must be killed says professor. *Times Educational Supplement* March 19th.

Swann, Lord (1985) *Education for All.* London: HMSO.

Tansley, P. , Nowaz and Roussou, M. (1985) *Working With Many Languages: A Handbook for Community Language Teachers.* London: School Curriculum Development Committee.

Taylor, M. (1986) *Chinese Pupils in Britain*. Windsor: NFER- Nelson.

Taylor, M. with Hegarty, S. (1985) *The Best of Both Worlds...? A Review of Research into the Education of Pupils of South Asian Origin*. Windsor: NFER-Nelson.

Thompson, A. (1991) *Exploring Bilingual Support in the Secondary School*. Hounslow Bilingual Support Project.

Tizard, B., Schofield, W. and Hewison, J. (1982) Collaboration between teachers and parents in assissting children's reading. *British Journal of Educational Psychology* 52, 1–15.

Tomlinson, S. (1984) *Home and School in Multicultural Britain*. London: Batsford.

— (1986) Ethnicity and educational achievement. In S. Modgil, G. Verma, R. Mallick and C. Modgil (eds) *Multicultural Education: The Interminable Debate* (pp. 181–94). Lewes: Falmer Press.

Tosi, A. (1988) The jewel in the crown of the modern prince: The new approach to bilingualism in multicultural education in England. In T. Skutnabb-Kangas and J. Cummins (eds) *Minority Education: From Shame to Struggle* (pp. 79–102). Clevedon, Avon: Multilingual Matters.

Townsend, H. (1971) *Immigrants in England: The LEA Response*. Windsor: National Foundation for Educational Research.

Townsend, H. and Brittan, E. (1972) *Organization in Multiracial Schools*. Windsor: National Foundation for Educational Research.

Troper, H. (1979) An uncertain past: Reflections on the history of multiculturalism. *TESL Talk* 10, 7–15.

Troyna, B. and Williams, J. (1986) *Racism, Education and the State*. London: Croom Helm.

Tsow, M. (1983) Analysis of responses to a national survey on mother- tongue teaching in LEAs 1980–2. *Educational Research* 25 (3), 202–8.

White, S.T. (1990) The Farsi speech community. In S. Alladina and V. Edwards (eds), Vol. 11, pp. 231–8.

Wiles, S. (1981) Language issues in the multicultural classroom. In N. Mercer (ed.) *Language in School and Community* (pp. 51–76). London: Edwards Arnold.

— (1985) Developments in ESL INSET: One centre's experience. In C. Brumfit *et al.* (eds), pp. 149–66.

Wolfendale, S. (1983) *Parent Participation in Children's Education and Development*. London: Gordon and Breach.

Wong, L. (1990) The Chinese speech community. In S. Alladina and V. Edwards (eds), Vol. 11, pp. 189–216.

Wright, C. (1986) School processes: An ethnographic study. In J. Eggleston (ed.) *Education for Some* (pp. 127–79). Stoke-on- Trent: Trentham.

Wright, E. (1971) *Program Placement Related to Selected Countries of Birth and Selected Languages*. Toronto: The Board of Education for the City of Toronto.

Wright, E. and Tsuji, G. (1984) *The Grade Nine Student Survey: Fall 1983*. Toronto Board of Education, Research Report No. 174.

York, G. (1989) *The Dispossessed*. Toronto: Lester and Orpen Dennys.

Index